Where you've never gone before . . .

The A.D.D. Quest for Identity

Inside the Mind of Attention Deficit Disorder

George H. Green, Ph.D.

Edited by Shirley L. Richardson

Third Edition

THE BiOFEEDBACK CENTER PRESS
Reno

Dedication

THIS brief book is dedicated to all the kids who might have contributed to society whom we have allowed to fall through the cracks. Their lost and countless numbers are the incalculable price we will always pay for insisting on conformity in education.

IT'S also dedicated to those who we suspect vanguarded the cause of ADD by their very existence and perseverance such as: Ben Franklin, Thomas Edison and Albert Einstein all of whom succeeded against odds and society's seeming demand for conformity.

DEDICATION of this work is also made to all of the researchers, educators and clinicians who believe in a brighter future in which all children will be able to celebrate their unique perspectives on life in such a manner that none will have to turn to the other side of the law to find understanding.

FINALLY, I wish to remember those very few teachers and professors who believed in me in their special way that resulted in my own perseverance even when I probably should have succumbed to the odds.

Acknowledgments

Some of the material in this book has appeared in the Reno Gazette-Journal and is used herein with their kind permission. Additionally, some material is used in my earlier book, **Life Without Stress: A Survival Guide**, and appears in **The A.D.D. Quest** in rewritten and substantially updated form to reflect new clinical perspectives on A.D.D.

Some of the components of this book were from scripts I wrote for and used in my Tuesday morning commentary on our local public radio station, KUNR, and I appreciate their continued support in this effort also.

Furthermore, most of the book is completely new, written to contribute new information and to tie together the numerous elements that make up this piece.

As a special acknowledgment, I received numerous gentle reminders from my friend and colleague, John Ziobro of Autogenics, Inc., to get this book completed. Apparently, I needed the push. Hopefully, this book will provide explanation for why.

For this Second Edition I am grateful to two people who have provided valuable critiques which have been excellent contributions and have reminded me that input from friends can make a substantial difference in life. Dr. Ed Lynn with his knowledge of myself and this subject made several suggestions that improved the accuracy of several key statements. Fran Elwell provided comments and an unprecedented in-depth proofreading.

Finally, on May 8, 1997 I introduced this book at a lecture I gave on A.D.D. I want to express thanks to the anonymous person who sought me out afterwards to comment, "You have A.D.D.! Well, that explains a lot!"

❦ Contents ❦

Introduction to the Third Edition
           Make no Comparisons   3
Table: Comparison of Bright, Gifted and
           Attention Deficit Disordered Students   4

SECTION ONE: **An ADD Case Study**   5
Chapter 1   7

SECTION TWO: **Inside the Need for Identity**   11
Chapter 2: The Quest for *Piece* of Mind   13
Chapter 3: A Simple Means of Identifying ADD   16
Chapter 4: A Close Look at Self-Identity   20
Chapter 5: The Quest for Identity Through Dreams   24
Chapter 6: Inside a Cartoon We Find Ourselves   28
Chapter 7: Cartoons Are Mirrors of Our Minds   32
Chapter 8: The Stresses We Find Inside   36
Chapter 9: Working With ADD and Stress   41

SECTION THREE: **Answers Inside the Mind of ADD**   45
Chapter 10: Deeper Inside the ADD Mind   46
Chapter 11: Getting an Attitude Adjustment   51
Chapter 12: Improving Attitude and Behavior   56
Chapter 13: Bringing Positivity into the Classroom   61
Chapter 14: Inside Getting Grades   66
Chapter 15: Creating Balance Inside the ADD Mind   70
Chapter 16: Reducing Stress Inside the ADD Family   77
Chapter 17: Implementing a Positive Environment   81
Chapter 18: Inside the Mind of a Winner   86

SECTION FOUR: **Inside the Mind and Biofeedback**   91
Chapter 19: Inside the Mind of the ADD Student *or*
            The Terror of Learning   92
Chapter 20: Defining the ADD Student and
            Defining a Solution   96
Chapter 21: Developing a Solution   101
Chapter 22: The Use of EEG Biofeedback
            (Neurofeedback) in Attention
            Deficit/Hyperactivity Disorder   105

SECTION FIVE: **Inside the ADD Mind**
            When the Negatives Win   115
Chapter 23: Fear Inside the Mind   116
Chapter 24: How to Get to the
            Wrong Side of the Law   125
Chapter 25: There's No Such Thing as Lazy   131
Chapter 26: Inside the ADD Criminal Mind   136

SECTION SIX: **Three Clinical Observations**   143
Chapter 27: ADD and Sleep   144
Chapter 28: Motivational Problems   149
Chapter 29: Teaching and Tutoring the ADD Student
            and Some Input on Ritalin™   158

SECTION SEVEN: **Inside Positive Communication** 163
Chapter 30: The Impact of Time Pressure   164
Chapter 31: Miscommunications   170
Chapter 32: A Journey Inside With My Son   174

SECTION EIGHT: **How to Be Positive With ADD**   179
Chapter 33: How to Be Positive with ADD   180

About the Author   186
Other Publications by Dr. Green   187

MAKE NO COMPARISONS

INTRODUCTION TO THE THIRD EDITION

An Oriental proverb tells us to:

> *Make no comparisons.*
> *Make no judgments.*
> *Delete the need to understand.*

Once inside the A.D.D. mind we see that these wise words are typically reversed. The person with A.D.D. always compares themselves to others . . . and always comes up short. Consequently, they are judging themselves against an impossible standard with the conclusion that they are somehow less than their peers.

As far as understanding is concerned, many, if not most, people with A.D.D. finally decide that their own perceptions of reality, which invariably differ from those of their peer group, are incorrect. Eventually they give up, their unique intellect and creativity lost to humanity.

The following table which has not appeared in past editions of this book was designed specifically to demonstrate the profound incorrectness of these assumptions. Be prepared to see A.D.D. from an entirely new perspective.

G.H.Green
Reno
February, 1998

Comparison of Intellectual Characteristics
of Students Who Are Bright, Gifted
and Attention Deficit Disordered

Bright*	Gifted*	ADD/ADHD**
Knows answers	Asks questions	Often afraid to ask
Interested	Curious about many subjects	Curious about many subjects
Attentive	Mentally/physically involved	Distracted by own thoughts
Good ideas	Wild, often silly ideas	Wild, often silly ideas
Works hard	Plays around yet tests well	Works hard or not at all
Copies accurately	Creates new design	Creates new design(s)
Listens with interest	Shows strong feelings	Strongly opinionated
Learns with ease	Already knows subject	Trouble presenting knowledge
Understands ideas	Constructs abstractions	Constructs abstractions
Good memorizer	Good guesser	Depends on guessing
Prefers structure	Thrives on complexity	Creates complexity
Technician	Inventor	Inventor
Alert	Observant	Observant when focused
Enjoys peers	Prefers more advanced	Creates path or leads others
Answers questions	Elaborates responses	Elaborates when focused
Grasps the meaning	Draws inferences	Draws inferences
Self-approving	Highly self-critical	Highly self-critical
Completes projects	Likes to experiment	Compulsive experimenter
Appreciates humor	Mature sense of humor	Very subtle sense of humor
Intelligent	Intelligent	Intelligent

* Source: Washoe County School District
** Source: The Biofeedback Center, Reno   © 1998, George H. Green, Ph.D., Reno

SECTION ONE

Inside
the Need
for Identity

CHAPTER ONE

LK was always considered bright, but he hated school. From first grade he had fits of anxiety making his mother drag him out from under his bed to meet the bus.

As time wore on, his anxieties became more subtle. He appeared to have gotten over whatever it was, but his grades remained low. LK's teachers continued telling him and his parents how bright he was as he continued to befriend his teachers rather than interact with his peers. When he did get involved with his peers, he stayed within a very small group except to get into trouble. Years later he confided to a counselor that he had no memories of ever feeling like he belonged in any school or even of being especially smart. He recalled how he insisted on inviting only adults to his eighth birthday party.

His grades got worse, but this was only a small part of the problem. His anxieties at school found expression at home as he felt increasingly isolated from his peers. Sarcasm and anger characterized much of his communications. With extreme dependence on his older brother, LK established self-doubt and low self-esteem as his strongest personality traits. "He could do better if only he tried," was the litany that accompanied him through the long, lonely halls of his academic career.

Serendipity played a significant role in his development. For as often as he got caught acting out, he was saved twice as often by circumstances. Teachers who caught him often ignored his behaviors. His one episode of shoplifting resulted in such a traumatic confrontation with the shop owner that he was actually *unable* to act out that way again. When LK was rejected by 18 colleges, the headmaster of his private school interceded and got him accepted to the college of a colleague of his. With his new found freedom, LK spent much of the first two years drinking. Then he quit college.

Afraid of disappointing his mother, LK agreed to go to a local university while living at home. This school had a special admissions policy: if you applied, you were accepted. At this point LK discovered drugs. His grades continued to be mediocre to horrible, and his social life was almost as dismal. In counseling he reported that he had no actual recollection of ever having spent time studying. The perplexing part was that LK was always eager to please. "I always intended to study. It just never happened." He learned not to raise his hand in class because he usually heard, "If you were paying attention, I just covered that a moment ago." He also developed annual anxiety attacks in August in painful anticipation of his return to school. This continued long after he left school behind.

He stayed in college only because he assumed that he would be unable to do anything else. "If I try, I'll just disappoint someone. I can't handle that." He spent more time on academic probation than off. Four years of college took six and a half.

"Jack of all trades, master of none."

"Work first, play later."

"Try hard and you can get A's."

"Head in the clouds."

"If you weren't so lazy, you could accomplish

anything you set your mind to."

LK devoted so much energy to rebelling against these repeated incantations that they became rigid structures in his life.

Despite all these hassles, or perhaps because of them, LK did reasonably well for himself. He never accomplished any of the pursuits he was expected to but rather made his own way, guided by some fortuitous happenstance as well as dogged obstinacy.

As it turns out, his school problems would be manageable today.

His problem? Attention Deficit Disorder. Who is LK? Me.

SECTION TWO

Inside
the Need
for Identity

CHAPTER TWO

The Quest
for *Piece* of Mind

The best way to get to know someone is to identify with that person. Although the case study was about myself, it has about it a feeling of commonality. I was surprised at how many elements, even details, of this study are repeated in the lives of dozens of the adults with whom I've worked who grew up with unidentified ADD.

The following section provides some insights into accurate identification of ADD. Rather than try to instruct you in making a clinical diagnosis (which has its own accuracy limitations anyway), you'll find anecdotal and experiential information designed to bring you closer to what it feels like to have ADD. It's laid out in some detail in order to assist you in developing an ADD perspective that you should be able to use as a pretty accurate identification system.

A quest is a wonderful thing.

It defines you.

It gives purpose to your life.

Merely making the decision to embark on a quest feels good in the sense of commitment it carries with it. A quest for identity is another matter entirely. Of the two basic questions of existence:

What is the meaning of life?
and
Who am I?

the former conjures up images of great debate and truly wondrous adventure while the latter connotes a sense of personal confusion, almost desperation.

However, what is it we all seek if not identity?

Our houses, our clothing, our choice of livelihood, our means of transportation, or the lack of any or all of these and innumerable other things comprise identity. If we feel we are without it, then we direct our full energy toward getting it.

Inside the *mind* of Attention Deficit Disorder.

Hopefully, this journey will be an unusual and elucidating experience. You may find *yourself* described in some detail in the pages that follow.

Either way you should be better prepared to

understand and work with people who have Attention Deficit Disorder and Attention Deficit Hyperactivity Disorder. Furthermore, it is hoped that you find personal solace as explanations for your own self-concerns are finally examined, explained and managed. As you read through these pages, you should either improve your ADD empathy or at least experience a sense of relief.

The purpose of *The A.D.D. Quest For Identity: Inside the Mind of Attention Deficit Disorder* has been to create a deeply personal understanding of both the perspectives that people with ADD have and the pressures they feel. What you will discover is that this problem, ADD, is easily comprehended by any who take the time to explore it. For most of us the qualities that create the differences that make up ADD are present, albeit in lesser degree. Furthermore, as for this book very practical suggestions are made about what can be done.

For the purposes of this book both Attention Deficit Disorder and Attention Deficit Hyperactivity Disorder are abbreviated as ADD. If I refer to one or the other specifically, I'll use the term that denotes the one to which I'm referring. I have also dropped the periods in the abbreviation for the sake of simplicity. Therefore, when you see ADD, think A.D.D. or A.D.H.D. depending on context. (If you shrewdly noticed the periods in the book title, I left them there since you hadn't read this chapter yet.)

Another convention I've chosen to use is placing a brief italicized section before each chapter. This allows me to make some informal comments about each topic that I either would like to emphasize or felt was important but didn't get stated in the chapter itself.

Since ADD affects males and females (about 3 to 1) as well as children and adults and since many of the qualities of ADD can be found in a large portion of the population, seeing life through the eyes of ADD should not be a daunting task. While my own observations indicate that males are affected by ADD about three times more often than females, a friend of mine who is a psychiatrist reports that his observations put this at two to one.

The A.D.D. Quest for Identity: Inside the Mind of Attention Deficit Disorder brings into our most personal spotlight the unique perspectives and filters that ADD imposes on the minds of those whose identity will always be a quest.

As we journey into these minds, your identity will never be in doubt. Try to recognize anyway the self-doubts and inner conflicts that characterize essentially every moment in these people's days. Take a few of your own moments to reflect on their feelings and perhaps identify with them, and you will likely find elements of yourself.

Some of this may be surprising, even shocking. Most of it should have the familiar ring of something that at least touched you deeply. The methods and techniques should have the comfortable rightness that accompanies logical thought.

These are not the mysteries of ADD. The enigma is based more on not looking closely enough than on understanding what we find when we get there.

The Quest, therefore, begins with an introspective breath. For in the mind of ADD you will find the need to be everyone. And in the mind of everyone resides the qualities of ADD.

Think of it as a roller coaster ride. You know you're OK, but it can still be a scary experience.

CHAPTER THREE

A Simple Means of Identifying ADD

This now begins the process of identifying with ADD. We are confronted with two forms of identification. Identification as a means of establishing the characteristics of an external phenomenon. And identification as an emotional bond with something. This next chapter is a very simple way to take that second feeling of identification and organize it into a means of recognition of ADD either in someone else or yourself.

A point worth repeating is as you consider the descriptive identification factors listed, you decide if they're all bad.

The most often asked question about ADD, second only to "Can they really be treated?" (Yes, they can.) is "How can I identify it?"

Aside from looking at the brainwaves for the peculiar patterns of ADD, the only other practical means of identification is behavioral observation.

Part of the confusion lies in two areas. First, the symptoms are, for the most part, exaggerations of "normal" personality characteristics. Second, it may not be so much a disorder as a different way of perceiving life. For these two reasons the ADD person may or may not be dysfunctional. When given the right circumstances, we tend to do pretty well. But I'm getting ahead of myself.

As you read the following description of typical ADD qualities, consider whether several of these qualities are part of your own make-up and whether they are really all that negative. Also, recent data indicates that a much larger percentage continue ADD into adulthood than had previously been suspected.

1. *Everything is top priority.* And it all needs to be done now. This continuous pressure produces a low level anxiety that pervades your reality.

2. *There's always at least a little hyper feeling.* No matter how hard you may try, it feels as if very little is accomplished so you never feel like you can truly rest. Often it boils down to "Why bother?" You're always one step away from feeling overwhelmed. Along with this comes chronic worrying.

3. *It's possible to get depressed with little or no provocation.*

4. *Intelligence is always an issue but rarely a problem.* You feel as if you can think real well but doubt it because it's so difficult to demonstrate. Eventually the frustration can stop you from even trying.

5. *For that matter you get frustrated very easily.* It's as if solutions are just out of reach, as if you already know how to play the game except someone changed the rules and told everyone else but you. Much of the time those around you will perceive your frustration as anger and react defensively.

6. *You excel at some things and crap out at the rest.* Actually, this is just performance. When you get motivated, you can do well at most things. It's just hard getting motivated when you feel your effort is not appreciated.

7. *You're preoccupied.* With several dozen ideas and thoughts swimming around in your consciousness simultaneously vying for the number one slot, creating the straightforward focus demanded by society becomes a nightmare.

8. *You're a maverick.* Never quite fitting in, you can appear very social only if you're in control of the situation. You're always most comfortable finding your own path through life. This need to express yourself uniquely can produce some shocking examples of creativity. Often you feel isolated.

9. *You're drawn to computers.* Not because they're logical, but because they provide a sort of instant gratification combined with intellectual challenge impossible to find elsewhere.

10. *No matter how old you get or what you end up doing, you can't get past the feeling of not knowing what you really want to do with your life.*

While this list does not comprise a medical diagnosis, these characteristics were compiled from working with dozens of people with ADD ranging from 7 to 57 years old including myself. If you found yourself described here, note that this configuration of qualities creates adaptability. With that can come the awareness that, if you manage to hang on, life can get a lot better.

CHAPTER FOUR

A Close Look
at Self-Identity

One of the most confusing characteristics of ADD is the "chameleon effect" wherein the person with ADD picks up their identity from the environment. This is an important part of the explanation for ADD kids' susceptibility to recruitment by gangs and resistance to punitive corrections. The driving need that burns so hotly inside their spirit will cause them to attach to literally anything that contributes to a feeling of belonging and approval

Don't forget that approval is also based on their interpretation and could mean anything. Even abject disapproval could be reinterpreted as approval if it contributed to self-identity.

When my son was 5 years old, he had become aware that I did a lot of writing and asked me what I was going to write about. "How some people have trouble really knowing who they are," said I sagaciously.

"How about you write about how brothers and sisters fight?" Same subject.

My son's identity at that moment was invested in fighting with his big sister. His ability to get her goat even at that tender age was exceptional, and he has dedicated a fair amount of energy in knowing how well he can do it. Self-identity has more to do with how we react than who we are. If you think you *are* your occupation, you're probably in need of some self-reassessing. Self-identity is, however, still wrapped up in those things we feel we do very well.

I like to think I'm a pretty good cowboy. This proves that self-identity does not have to agree with reality.

Not all qualities found in your self-identity are necessarily beneficial. If you have trouble accepting your own good qualities, your self-identity can contain characteristics that will be personally detrimental.

The great difficulty focusing their attention that brings about poor academic performance and poor self-esteem despite above average intelligence found in ADD leads to personal stress partly because they're told they could perform if they would only try and partly because this tends to isolate them from their peer group.

Archetypal ADD sufferers simply can't hold their focus the way society expects them to. They exist in a world where everyone else seems to know what's expected except them.

Fertile ground for an identity crisis.

As I've said repeatedly, these individuals usually struggle to create an identity, as we all do, that's unique. Unfortunately, they usually can't find it in anything that involves structure such as academics. They commonly discover that they get attention, and hence identity, by acting out. Since this provides an important outlet for their frustrations, it gets reinforced. Frequently, and this was how I did it, they learn that the longer they take to do anything, not just those things that are difficult for them, but anything, the more important they become by delaying other people.

Outwardly, I used to be angered when my big brother called me "Take-a-year", but inwardly I knew I held a certain control by being slow. I've seen this in several of the people with whom I have worked who have had ADD. It's not a beneficial trait to be sure, but it makes you important anyway, and that's what we seek. Importance, uniqueness, self-identity.

Self-identity is a complicated blend of dozens of characteristics that run concurrently in the background of our minds jumping to the front only as needed or challenged. If you're dealing with someone who is annoying to you, you're dealing directly with their self-identity.

If you find yourself stuck in a pattern that you know is not good but feel helpless to stop, you've found one of your own self-identity qualities.

Before trying to change or upgrade our self-identity, it is essential that we simply observe ourselves and those around us. Learn to understand when you feel you're being compromised. As you gain awareness about yourself and others, talk with someone you trust about what both of you have learned about yourselves. Ways to grow will become evident as you start to see yourself through the eyes of that other person.

By learning to do this you put yourself in a position to empathize with both the ADD person *and* their self-image.

When I ride the range, if you run into me out there, the chances are that I won't say, "Hi."

I'll probably say, "Howdy."

CHAPTER FIVE

The Quest for Identity Through Dreams

Yet another aspect of ADD that creates problems is the tendency to be introspective. Introspection, in and of itself, is harmless enough. It can be a very productive behavior and the seed of considerable creativity. It can and does refresh the mind. It can even bring deeper understanding of how we grow and help us to direct our lives.

Unless it becomes a full-time job.

For ADD brings with it introspection as a preoccupation. Introspection as not just a means but often as the end or object of those means as well. Most ADD's (shorthand for people with ADD) are very creative individuals indeed, but the strength of their self-doubts usually blocks their ability and need to express their creative urges.

From this most likely springs the reputation that ADD's are dreamers.

One morning while driving to my office I saw something that probably should have provided no more than a passing thought. But I couldn't get the image out of my mind. Here and there lying along the road near no one's house in particular were Christmas trees. Apparently dumped roadside, tinsel and all, as an expeditious solution to an annoying problem. At the time I couldn't clearly identify just why this was so discomfiting. But it stayed with me. We had just come through the tragic New Year's Flood of '97, and you'd think we'd want to hold on to dreams or symbols of dreams.

Or at the least give them more respect than a roadside dumping.

As it happened, I had also recently been discussing the plight of kids with ADD in our social system. Often discarded as behavioral problems or unable to make the kind of grades that would reflect their true intelligence, I couldn't help identifying these kids with the discarded trees. Things of beauty that just couldn't fit in.

Just a few days later a friend of mine was telling me of the passing of one of her patients who had such profound faith that she held on to life way beyond the limits of medical science. A few weeks earlier my neighbor of eighteen years experienced the same thing with his wonderful wife. Both of these fine women have gone on to their rewards. Their memories in juxtaposition with the flood and these discarded trees have caused me to look inward past the platitudes and well wishes to find some meaning of these things that give me pause.

ADD creates introspection as you try to make sense of the barrage of data that you rarely seem to be able to process to the liking of those in positions to judge us. Necessarily and as a function of a greater tendency to defocus or become distracted, ADD produces dreamers. While there is no way to document this directly, Benjamin Franklin, Thomas Edison and Franz Schubert are all suspected of having been ADD.

On the day the flood started, I watched a fellow Posse member rescue an older woman from a stranded car. I listened as one of my ranch partners told me of walking in thigh deep water to bring our horses to high ground. And I worried with my partners as we awaited news of our other livestock that had to wait out the water's rise and eventual recession on their own.

For me there are so many dreams in life that at times it seems that's all I have. As a matter of fact, I've been told I was too much of a dreamer since I was a child. I guess I haven't grown out of it. Since it's probably linked to the ADD, I presumably won't. But I personally cannot think of a better way to exalt the future than with dreams. For that matter, what better way to exalt life?

These women who've passed on were

dreamers. And their dreams gave them life. In the face of disaster, my friend, Brad, risked hypothermia for our horses. He must have dreamt a future also. And Posse member, Paula, couldn't ignore that car in the water past its hubs. My friend, Carrie, was so touched by her patient that her life has changed and now mine as well. My neighbor, Martin, shared over a half a century with a woman who not only shared his dreams but gave so much substance to them that they persist even after she's gone.

And the image of those unceremoniously discarded trees finally came into focus for me. I feel sorry for the owners of those trees, but in my experience they are the minority. I am most fortunate to be surrounded by dreamers who have found and are finding their sense of future each in their own way but with one important common thread.

We dream.

And in our dreams reside hope and potential, faith and love. A universe of maybe's that is just enticing enough to keep our interest.

I hope I never discard old dreams.

And I plan to continue to keep fellow dreamers close to me. Perhaps my greatest accomplishments have been a direct product of my ability, my *need*, to imagine.

Smoke in the wind? I think not. Beacons to the future and meaning to a life that I can wrap my arms around and from which I get some surprisingly special smiles.

If it's ADD, then it might just be an asset.

CHAPTER SIX

Inside a Cartoon We Find Ourselves

Now we move out of the realm of dreams into that realm created intentionally by us. In some ways this realm is more real than reality in that it holds gross exaggerations of reality as cartoonists create characters by holding up a clown house mirror to our psyches and reporting what they see. Rather than distortions their mirrors render reality in an almost too real perspective.

It is from this vantage point that the cartoonists have captured something I had missed for years: the pervasiveness of ADD qualities in cartoon characters. Why this is so is the subject of the next two chapters. Why this is important is that by laughing at our faults we acknowledge their presence and attempt to process a means of resolving them.

Sometimes I turn to unusual places for guidance. This time I'm asking you to follow me into the brain of Bart Simpson.

One of my important discoveries, while on my way to the brain, was that his heart is most definitely in the right place. This is significant in the light of further findings.

Bart has Attention Deficit Hyperactivity Disorder. You know the drill: the inability to maintain concentration, poor grades in school, impulsive behaviors resulting in personal risk, excessive aggressiveness with peers, poor self esteem, social behavior below his chronological age, above average intelligence. He can be surprisingly creative when working on something that holds his interest. All in all, he is one of the most extreme cases I've seen. And for all his seemingly antisocial qualities, he desperately wants to fit in, be liked and perform normally. Despite sometimes Herculean efforts on his part, he just can't make it.

We can assume that the creator and writers of the Simpsons did not deliberately describe a child having problems due to ADHD. The amazing thing is that they have created someone we could relate to easily, and they did it with uncanny accuracy. By exaggerating difficulties they created an immensely popular cartoon character. One of my clinical colleagues believes that some degree of ADHD affects a very large portion of our society. I know I see parts of myself in Bart and Homer. (I'm not saying which parts.)

In the time that I have been working with Attention Disorders, I have spoken with many parents and colleagues. Practically every one can recognize aspects of the dysfunction in themselves. Perhaps not to the extent that it became a great hinderance in their lives, but still unmistakably there. And they know it.

I'm not asking you to like the Simpsons or even to watch the show. Just consider the ramifications. To function in our society you must conform to certain expectations of behavior. This includes going through a structured school system for upwards of a decade and a half, spending countless hours in diligent studying and listening.

Many dedicated teachers struggle within this system for student attention that often seems disturbingly elusive. Grappling with minds that get saturated or distracted long before the bell rings or the book gets read takes its toll on teachers and students alike. I wonder how many people with test anxiety are actually poorly prepared because they cannot hold their focus either when studying or during tests.

In one episode of the Simpsons, Bart fought valiantly against a merciless barrage of distractions as he actually tried to study. He was helpless against his father's expectations to watch TV together ("Maybe just one more hour, then I gotta hit the books."). Locking himself in the basement to avoid the temptations of a surprise snow storm, wild unrelated thoughts invaded his mind. I'm not excusing his behavior, but it can be explained and even helped.

If I could check Bart's brainwaves, I'm pretty sure what we'd find. And then, with appropriate training and some positive reinforcement, his grades could improve. With his focus improving, impulsive and inappropriate behaviors would subside as his self-esteem began to strengthen.

He would probably lose his job as a cartoon character, but he'd be on the road to a pretty good life.

CHAPTER SEVEN

Cartoons Are Mirrors of Our Minds

Going beyond Bart Simpson we find the ubiquitous quality of ADD reflected in such a wide range of make believe characters that the possibility of ADD being common in the general public is very strong. Rather than approaching this as a dysfunction requiring special attention, perhaps we could begin the slow process of improving our educational process so that all students would benefit.

It's happening so much, it's a phenomenon.

When I made the observation that Bart Simpson had ADHD and that it was likely to have been inherited from his father, Homer, who displayed similar, if more obnoxious, symptoms, it was intended to demonstrate the ubiquitousness of the ADD symptoms. Bart regularly demonstrates extreme impulsivity (when he destroyed his sister's handmade Thanksgiving centerpiece to make room for the turkey), easy distractibility (when he gets distracted in school by anything), inappropriate social behaviors (when he leads other kids in playing hookey), the need for constant stimulation (Bart's life is a frenetic adventure from one problem to the next.) as well as other symptoms.

When I looked at other comic cartoon characters, however, I was amazed by what I discovered. Since I don't know how to adapt my biofeedback equipment to working with two-dimensional people, we'll have to content ourselves with these few observations that unfortunately have no electroencephalographic data to back it up.

Calvin of the Calvin & Hobbes team has a marvelous imagination that constantly drags him away from reality especially when that reality has to do with school. He's not stupid. Quite the opposite; he just can't demonstrate his intelligence in a socially acceptable format. This, of course, is common to most ADD & ADHD people.

Frank & Ernest, and even Beetle Bailey, find themselves cast off by a society they seem to understand all too well but in which they do not fit.

Dennis the Menace is definitely hyperactive with enough impulsivity and creative overdrive to make even Bart look tame.

Poor Andy Capp can't keep a job, impulsively pursues the ladies, speaks without any thought of consequence and seems to have a casual attitude toward hygiene. Most of these characters push deadlines to the limit and beyond giving them a reputation for lateness.

As interesting as these discoveries were, the one that impressed me most was Peanuts. Three of the members of this little community stand out as having ADD beyond question.

First, there's Peppermint Patty. A maverick who must always be in charge to cover her fear of rejection, she can't even focus long enough to hand in her homework in school. In fact, the most common cartoon frame is of her sitting at her school desk with her head flopped all the way back, snoring. Her mind is just too busy to be bothered with the snail's pace of traditional education.

Then there's Good Ol' Charlie Brown. He represents the ultimate outcast of a society that can't figure out what to do with him. Desperately desiring to fit in and make friends, it is the one thing he just can't manage. He's smart enough to make it into spelling bees and other intellectual competitions, but invariably can't perform under pressure. His self-esteem is so damaged that he assumes no one really wants to like him and that he'll probably fail at whatever he attempts. He cannot fathom cause-and-effect so he invariably makes his mistakes over again . . . especially when kicking the football.

Perhaps the quintessential example of the ADHD in all of us, however, is Snoopy. Hyperactive to a fault, he has no control whatsoever of his actions or impulsivity. He defies authority as a way of life, conforming to the demands of society just long enough to get his supper bowl filled. His imagination is second to none, and his best friend, Woodstock, is not only another societal outcast but is so much smaller than Snoopy that his presence helps Snoopy feel useful and effective.

There are two messages here.

1) ADD must be so common that to reflect reality these comics recognize those aspects of our daily lives we tend to ignore.

2) I'm going to have to let my kids read comics more often since *I'm* apparently not about to stop.

CHAPTER EIGHT

The Stresses
We Find Inside

Yet another problem inherent within the mind of ADD is the assumption that you'll screw up just because you have in the past. This type of patterning can be a potent negative force that acts as a self-fulfilling prophecy. This carries rational problems due to the ADD into the non-affected portion of the person's existence. This generalizing effect is likely the cause of many gross behavioral dysfunctions that show up years after the ADD makes its initial manifestations.

I hated school.

No, that's not exactly true. I feared it. It was the place I went to be reminded that I was not the A student my parents said I should be. It was where I had trouble making friends. It was where I got into trouble despite my best efforts not to. It was where my ADD defined and confined my reality like no schoolyard bully ever could.

But this isn't about that.

This is the 103rd piece I've written on the subject of stress. I'm impressed. My academic career was not noted for this level of productivity. Actually, deadlines for me produced the kind of terror redolent with attacks of sleepless anxiety. In school and college I would put off writing papers until the last possible second then scramble like mad to produce something meaningful. Producing something meaningful at 3:00 A.M. after staring at a blank piece of paper for four hours can be a trifle tricky. So I'd dress up my paper with some pithy quote that I brilliantly located in "Bartlett's Familiar Quotations" after a lengthy two or three minute search. Since I'm sure no one else ever thought of doing this, feel free to use it.

I've since managed to graduate (much to the

extreme pleasure of several teachers to be rid of me at last).

The issue here is that annually I would ruin my entire month of August with the anticipation of how awful school would be. Whenever I thought of Labor Day and the inevitable return to the "salt mines" as my dear mother used to refer to them, my stomach would knot up, and I'd get depressed. Before you present me with the Woody Allen Award For Neurotic Introspection, look at what motivates this type of reaction.

"Sure," you might say, "school was tough so you had negative anticipations about returning to that toughness." That's certainly part of it, but there's more to it than that.

ADD fosters the creation of negative anticipations based on assumptions. This is a dangerous practice at best. But with ADD, of course, danger is rarely an aversive issue.

It's also so common that we all do it every day.

It's far easier to assume something will happen than to research it fully enough to actually find out if it will. Most of the time we couldn't find out even if we tried. So we assume it will happen . . . especially if it's negative.

It's not the anticipation itself that's causing the problem. It's the basic presumption. It's built on a non-existent premise. I was recently talking with a client about this topic. She has ADD and had returned to school feeling stressed. After thinking it through, she discovered that there was very little reason to be stressed. She had come to terms with her ADD and had found that she could accomplish more by being relaxed than being tense. She also discovered that she had to become specific about whose opinions she would value. Good advice for anyone, but especially good advice with ADD. She had found, much to her surprise, that she had been feeling stressed because she had *assumed she would* based solely on her years of negative comments and poor grades.

Her current performance was acceptable to her, and her new found confidence did not include allowing herself to feel judged. After due consideration, she let herself relax and got down to the task of being a student. And actually enjoyed it.

I wonder how many of my hassles in school were of my own doing simply because I expected those hassles to be there. It's a little scary to consider that I may have even invented a lot of them.

Products of my overactive ADD imagination combined rather successfully with my unpleasant experiences to create a future reality so potent that I'm not sure I could have had a good time if it had occurred..

My memory tells me they were all real, but I wonder. And how many Augusts were needlessly ruined?

I may be a little neurotic, but at least I can make a couple of points with it. One is the presumption that misery inevitably creates a miserable experience. ADD leads us into so much of this it can become a habit for both the person with ADD and the family. You not only get to worry about it for a month in advance, but you can also be miserable afterwards.

And nothing stressful need ever happen.

The other point? I got to brag about all my writing. And *that's* been *wonderful* for my self-image.

CHAPTER NINE

WORKING WITH ADD AND STRESS

Clinically, we define stress as "an over-reaction to a perceived stimulus."

Each word of this definition is important here. "Over" states directly that a stress response is too much. It is more than is needed to manage whatever we perceive the stress to be. "Reacting" means saving your life for in reality a stress response is your body's, and indeed your mind's, reaction to perceived dire threat to life.

So an over-reaction is quite directly too much of a good thing or even a completely inappropriate response altogether. The latter is generally the case.

For the parents or teachers working with ADD kids, a stress response is unfortunate, but common. There is rarely, if ever, a dire threat to life. Yet blood pressures rise, hostility and self-image become issues, and in the process of behaving as if some opposing tribe were attacking our cave the real issue, the ADD, is forgotten.

I'd hope that we've advanced a little more than that over the past several millennia.

For the person with ADD, the perception of dire threat, while still over-reactive, is actually closer to reality since their perceived place in life feels challenged.

This, then, is the nature of the pressure that drives the ADD individual. The next chapter deals directly with the beginnings of handling this problem.

Not enough time. Not enough energy. Not enough recognition. Not enough love.

Many people with ADD tell me they feel like they overreact to just about everything in their lives. While they are aware their feelings and reactions are excessive, they feel caught, unable to find their way to the top of the pile.

When you end up in this unpleasant state, you feel as if everything in your life is vying for top priority, and you don't have time to get it all done.

What's worse, the only item at the bottom of the priority list is yourself.

With ADD these extremes get demonstrated with impulsive behaviors that produce a wide range of unfortunate outcomes. Bursts of anger. Suddenly asking for a divorce. Quitting a job without thinking it through. Running away. Getting involved in substance abuse.   And these are just a few possibilities from a wide range.

If you feel like doing these sort of things but don't act on them, this can diminish the impact of your feelings and the need for resolution. It means you are still in control. You may, however, be storing the unresolved feelings. Some form of expression is generally a good idea. Just talking about it can be a far more powerful release than many people are aware. The act of voicing your feelings *and* sharing them with another human being can cue your subconscious to let go of the tension that's building up.

If, on the other hand, you find yourself merely exaggerating your responses to everyday hassles, you are probably overwhelmed.

This problem occurs when you have no place to retreat emotionally. When every corner of your life is in a state of change or when you feel life's demands pushing your sense of reality toward over-stimulation. When everyone and everything seems to depend on your time, you feel trapped.

Imagine feeling that your job is not fulfilling and that everyone expects you to take care of everything. Add to that the fact that money is tight and the bills are paid late. Now consider that the kids or the dogs need attention. When that's done, you can start on the house. You try to get energy from your relationship, but your partner isn't responding. Then you get a traffic ticket and drop into a deep depression.

When you are overwhelmed, it feels like there's no place to hide.

And the ADD mind spends most of the time overwhelmed. Here are some perspectives and techniques that can get you started managing your reality a little better.

Solutions:

Start by creating effective priorities. In reality, you can only work on one thing at a time. In the ADD mind everything fights for attention simultaneously, but you can only work with one. Find out what is really impending. Resolve it or set it aside as circumstance dictates and go on to the next thing.

Remember, *you* are the top priority in your life.

If you do not care for yourself, you will not be able to care for others. Furthermore, if you do not care for yourself, learning how to prioritize will be a monumental task. If you put yourself last, that's not humility, that's foolishness. Such reduced self-esteem can and does diminish the quality of your work and your life.

Set aside time for yourself. However little, it must be yours. Depend on it. Make it happen. Then label it when it does happen: "This feels nice." "I deserve this." These can be simple things. Go for a walk. Exercise. Window-shop. Enjoy a sunset.

Living with ADD teaches us, erroneously, that our opinions don't count. That the only way to make an impression is forcibly or not at all.

If we are to believe that everyone is important, then we must learn to include ourselves. Time for yourself is the best way to learn self-nurturing.

And do it without guilt.

"I don't have time for that." Make the time. It's essential. And it works.

I'm not advocating irresponsibility. I'm suggesting a higher level of responsibility, one that includes you, the person, instead of you, the poor martyr.

Corny? You bet. Effective? Right again.

SECTION THREE

Answers
Inside the Mind
of ADD

CHAPTER TEN

Deeper Inside the ADD Mind

We all know the difference between negative and positive. Or at least we all think we know.

As we extend our exploration inside the ADD mind, the impact of both the internal influence of the ADD and the external influence of a well-intended teacher combine as a dramatic and devastating force. The effect of this force is the lowering of the motivation of the ADD student. Even lowering self-expectations

Inside the mind of ADD we see that after repeated negative experiences the mind can no longer justify the effort needed to vindicate itself.

It's a short step from here to loss of direction.

"OK, here I am in Math class. Mr. Melrose said we'd better learn this stuff because it's going to be on the test next week. I've got to pull up my grade, or I'll get pulled off the track team. Today I'm going to focus. Every single word he says I am going to hear. Alright, here he comes."

Perhaps the most paradoxical aspect of Attention Deficit Disorder is that most of the time significant effort goes into doing the right thing. In this case it's mentally preparing for class. The intent is there. . . for now.

"This seat is so uncomfortable. It must have been made for munchkins. If I were making school seats, I'd pad them. Yeah, pad them and maybe make them in a few sizes so . . . Hey! When did he start his lecture? I'm behind, and I haven't even started. It's always like this. Look at those other guys. They always seem to know just what's going on. And those girls up front! How do they do it? Uhoh, what's he doing now? Where've I been? He's ten minutes into the class, and I don't know what he's talking about. This is nothing new. I don't know why I bother. Alright already, focus! I have got to focus!"

Good intentions give way to anxiety fairly quickly as the person with ADD realizes they're not functioning at the same level as their peers.

The A.D.D. Quest for Identity　　　　**47**

Frequently, the harder they try, the worse their focusing gets. Parents, teachers, counselors often try to encourage these students by saying, "You can do it if you'd just try," or "Try harder," or "Until your grades come up, you can't stay on the track team." Each of these well-intended remarks may very well have the effect of provoking more effort, but unfortunately for most people with ADD the increased effort is met with increased *de*focusing.

"He's doing something with square roots. I hate square roots! Who invented those things? And who came up with that crazy division sign? Looks like a two dimensional can opener for two dimensional cans. What would that be? A two dimensional can, hmmm. That would just be a 'U'. Yeah, it would look like a letter 'U' because you couldn't have sides without a third dimension. Oh no! Where'd all those equations on the board come from? I'm really in for it now. I'll never figure out what he's talking about."

Most people with ADD seem to be pretty intelligent. But between being easily distracted and losing focus when they try to apply themselves, demonstrating that intelligence becomes a harrowing task usually met with failure.

"Oh, good Lord, he's calling on me! Yes, Mr. Melrose. No, sir, I don't know. Could you repeat the question? No, sir, I wasn't sleeping. No, I'm not trying to be a wise guy. Thank you for repeating the question. Ummm, no, I guess I don't know the answer."

And with that failure comes humiliation. It's not far from there to loss of self-esteem. It's not so much that their mind wanders as that the wandering is provoked by the very effort they're being asked to make. Even worse is that the mind-wandering effect is provoked by the efforts they are *trying* to make in good faith. So they comply with requests to pay attention, but in so doing they actually defocus. You ask them to repeat what you just said, and they can't. They get embarrassed or angry both of which are inappropriate. This further frustrates the people working with them which can evoke demonstrations of anger on *their* part. The person with ADD now feels punished either for no reason or because, in their mind, they feel stupid.

"No, Mr. Melrose, I don't know where I was just now. I thought I was listening to you. No, I suppose I wasn't. Yes, I'm aware that I'm failing, and I need to pull up my grade."

Self-deprecation is common, and it can surface as over-compensating hostility or acting out in other ways. This over-compensation makes them feel effective, functional and noticed. Even if it's antisocial behavior, it becomes an identity. One that provides a powerful and needed sense of security that even the best intentions by the adults in their support system cannot offset.

"I don't know why I bother. It's always the same old thing. Now I have to face my parents. That's gonna be fun! They must think I'm some kind of idiot. I must be. Now I can't even be on the track team.

What's the use . . ."

As I've worked clinically with ADD, I've found that patience is preeminent followed closely by understanding what might be going through their minds. Attention Deficit Disorder is accompanied by a *profound need for identity*. In the case I related just now being encouraged to remain on the track team would have provided more emotional energy for possibly improving grades than being taken off. Trying to hammer knowledge into their heads or removing activities that benefit their self-image provides marginal success at best. But providing a positive environment in which can be found both identity and stimulation can access their intelligence. Once accomplished a well-spring of creativity is often found.

For the person with ADD trying harder and harder until it finally works isn't going to produce positive results. Feeling good about themselves and being comfortable with who they are is more likely to lead to success. A new way of teaching is required that emphasizes self-respect and recognizes the power and value of individuality.

It won't be easy, but the curious thing about these changes is that the old ways benefit only the portion of the population that is *not* ADD. These new ways have the potential of reaching almost everyone.

CHAPTER ELEVEN

Getting an
Attitude Adjustment

Shifting from negative to positive can be a staggering task.

In this chapter we'll look at the most common school stress experienced by an ADD student. Note that inside the mind the first steps toward self-deprecation are taken and perceptually reinforced.

Unless those people in the ADD person's support group are informed of these emotional processes, their well-intended help will have the reverse effect.

I'm pretty introspective as it is, but since ADD affects me so personally, writing about it puts me in an even more thoughtful place.

In the midst of my thoughts (*"I could have done that better." "I wish I had spent more time with that person." "I want to spend more time with my kids." "Why didn't I ever pursue music writing?"*), it occurred to me that I was being a little negative. Actually, I was being a lot negative. I spoke to a couple of friends about this, and they assured me that I was indeed negative, and I needed to learn to like myself more.

"How?!" I replied. No one wants to be told they don't like themselves. Especially if it may be true. Of course, with ADD the issue of self-liking can be an everyday battle.

"When's the last time you said something nice about yourself to someone else without feeling guilty?"

This question became increasingly depressing as I continued to think about it. Another typical ADD quality. So I talked to more people.

"I'm nice to myself." I was told, "Check out my wheels. Sixty payments and it's mine!" Unconvinced, I ventured on. "I have no trouble being nice to myself. I exercise daily, try to eat right, get all my work done on time." "But what do you do just for yourself?" "No time for that! Besides, all *that* stuff's bad for me."

I kept at my inquiries until I'd hammered together a theory, "The Theory of Negativity". With a name like that it had to be great.

I concluded that we all maintain a staff of internal judges. With ADD they are especially critical. They never assess anything based on its own value. Relative value is all that matters. Not, "How well did you do?" Just, "Who came in first?" Next to the best and you may as well be last.

We're pummeled with facts like which state has the most suicides or which state has the best schools. Or who's the class valedictorian. Or which analgesic lasts longest. So we do it to ourselves. Even news stories are purposefully rewritten using the phrase, "For the *first* time in four years..." Instead of saying, "The last time this occurred was four years ago..." The notion of being first or best carries with it the impression of the epitome of importance.

This mentality applies incredible pressure to the person with ADD who may very well be bright enough but isn't able to perform in precisely the expected manner. Since they step to a different beat, often there's very little patience or appreciation for the efforts they make. There are no real prizes for trying regardless how hard.

Society has a new Golden Rule: A gold medal is something to remember; silver's good for the moment; bronze is forgotten. And those who tried never existed.

I suggest some modifications to the way we

communicate:

"The following states have reduced their suicides."

"These states are maintaining schools of high standards."

"These students get a lot of credit for trying hard."

"Different analgesics affect people differently."

Negative recognition, however, is readily available. Drive too fast and get a ticket. Smoke that and go to jail. Break a rule and get punished. We've got over a million people in prison in the United States. To how many people have we given permission to feel good about themselves? We applaud the Chef for a Blue Ribbon meal. The dishwasher goes unnoticed even though *he's* the one who's protecting our health. If we do a good job, we're given a cursory "That's nice." How about special recognition for kids who manage to get B's and C's and don't get into trouble? I spent more time in detention than I did getting appreciation. But I was told often enough that I should be shooting for the A's.

The son of a friend of mine got straight F's on his report card. He's a good kid. Actually, he's a terrific kid, but he's responding to some serious life stresses plus his ADHD. I managed to get him into some counseling which is helping his self-esteem. The next report card came back with only 3 F's and some C's and D's. I was thrilled and told him so. He made an effort, and it showed. Most of the time he's still down on himself, however, because most of the people with whom he's interacting only see his failure. He ends up hating himself, and for what?

At the end of the next marking period with some counseling and some special tutoring he'd managed to pull his grades up. A couple of F's, a couple of D's and a C.

Now here's where the system falls apart.

His mother successfully praised him for his effort (which was substantial from ADD standards) as did his tutor. His father practically read it off a script, "More bad grades! I thought you were trying to improve." At least one of his teachers did manage to acknowledge that some progress was made.

So now he's back to struggling again. He's back to being self-deprecating because that's what he was instructed to do by his adult models.

I still have trouble appreciating myself. I was at a meeting recently and saw a bullwhip hanging on the wall. Next to it was a sign, "This will continue to be used until your attitude improves!"

The Theory of Negativity states that if a little punishment doesn't strengthen your self-esteem, then a lot will surely work.

The student I talked about in this chapter is no stranger to the emotional bullwhip.

And the worst part is that he thinks he deserves it.

CHAPTER TWELVE

Improving Attitude and Behavior

Now we start developing the positive qualities that are such an essential part of working with ADD.

Making these changes may seem at first to be an immense task, and the responses that appear will probably be quite subtle, but over time with practice they will become increasingly easy and increasingly obvious.

Just as with correcting any behavior, replacing negative comments, especially the hard-to-see ones, with positive comments will initially feel stilted. But as the new behaviors are introduced and the person with ADD starts to feel better about themselves, all people involved will find that being positive is not only easier but self-nurturing as well.

"I told you to get off the phone an hour ago! Just for that you're grounded Saturday."

"If you keep your grades up until summer, you can travel with your friends."

"So you finally got around to doing those chores. It's about time!"

"So you got a job, and now you feel big. When you can save your money, then I'll be impressed."

These are negative statements that send demeaning and potentially devastating messages to the receiver. Basically, it's all one message: "No matter how good you get, it's never going to be good enough."

These messages *masquerade* as effective parenting while actually just massaging our parental insecurities. Ultimately, they actually *strengthen* the negative behavior we're trying to squelch by forcing the child or adolescent into a resentment that literally encourages them to resort to these same behaviors in an effort to strengthen their self-identity.

While this is true in any relationship in which one person is the role model for another, it's especially applicable when responding to those with ADD. Since, as I've pointed out, most ADD behaviors manifest commonly in us to some degree (impulsiveness, lack of understanding consequence, feelings of not fitting in, defiance of authority, difficulty setting priorities), modifying these disciplinary methods can be of benefit to virtually anyone and certainly to any relationship.

Until you get the hang of it, however, finding a way to strengthen someone's ego while reinforcing the need for discipline is a conundrum. To be positive *without negativity* while exerting a negative force *positively* can be as difficult to conceptualize as it is to say.

Recognize that the children or adolescents you're trying to help have already heard and processed all the negatives you can generate. Continued repetition may give you the illusion of doing something affirmative, but the object of this well-intentioned harangue (the child or adolescent) has already heard it all, probably from you and most likely just yesterday. Their minds, and certainly the ADD mind, manage quite successfully to shut out these messages by the time you're just getting warmed up based solely on your tone of voice.

Therefore, no yelling.

Not even that special controlled voice that says through clenched teeth, "I may not be yelling, but you can be damn certain I *want* to!" Recognize right now that getting riled up will only contribute to the very problem you're trying to correct.

Be positive.

Here are the statements made above converted to be more positive and supportive while carrying greater corrective force.

"I know you've been trying to be better about

the phone, and you have been, but right now you've lost track of time."

"Next summer I think you'll be mature enough to travel with your friends. By the way I see how hard you've been working on your grades."

"Thanks for doing those chores. Nice work!"

"Congratulations on landing that job. Would you like help setting up that savings account?"

These may not give you the *immediate* correction you seek, but those old corrective patterns yield nothing while these represent a reasonable start. Now it's essential that you notice any movement in the correct direction regardless of how small and *acknowledge it.*

"I noticed your phone conversations are getting shorter. Thanks." This applies even if the decrease is 2 minutes.

"I know you're not doing as well as you'd like in History, but I want you to know I'm aware how hard you're trying, and I'm impressed." Even if the last grade was a D.

"I noticed you took out the garbage yesterday. Thanks for saving me the hassle."

"Keep up those interviews. It's only a matter of time before an employer sees your strengths as I do."

If there's one thing I've learned in treating Attention Deficit Disorder, it's that *you can't fool the ADD mind.* They're perceptive, and they're bright. Poor grades and discipline problems have very little to do with true intelligence.

It's good advice to mean what you say when you talk with people who have ADD.

Once you're caught in a deception, you've compromised your credibility.

Honesty also opens the door for other types of nurturing communications which leads to maturation, a sense of responsibility and, ultimately, a stronger and healthier self-identity.

CHAPTER THIRTEEN

Bringing Positivity Into the Classroom

When I teach, I notice that on days when I'm in a good mood I see very little yawning in my classes. Conversely, on days when I'm tired or upset about something, I have trouble keeping my students' interest. Similarly, I find students' questions that cause me to repeat myself are more common when I don't feel vivacious in class.

A friend of mine was criticized for a teaching style that "had him all over the room like a high school physics teacher." By this I assume that meant he was animated and excited about his subject (political science).

He was voted best teacher of the year so I guess that's a point in favor of high school physics teachers.

I really like having cable TV. I can relive shows from my childhood. And the movie channels can be educational.

Maybe I'd better explain that last comment.

One evening I was channel surfing for my definition of some basic entertainment: science fiction or mindless violence. Not finding either of those I was drawn in to a movie that I couldn't follow. Well, since they had British accents, I figured I might get some culture indirectly.

Imagine my surprise when that's what happened.

After about a half-hour of bizarre vignettes a dapper individual in his thirties appeared before a backdrop of stars and began singing what I later learned was The Galaxy Song. It was terrific. With a simple vamp tune he regaled us, with remarkable accuracy I might add, with facts astronomical. It was fascinating to hear all that hard science slide effortlessly through the vehicles of the music and the movie.

It turned out I had been watching Monty Python's "Meaning of Life". I had watched Monty Python and gotten educated! I was enchanted.

You see, I've been hammering away for years that both teaching *and* learning should be fun. Not just for ADD, but for everyone. I've had quite a few arguments about this, but I'm adamant. Both the processes of learning and that of teaching should and can be enjoyable, stimulating and, well, fun. Think back to your most memorable teachers. The ones you recall in a positive light.

As I've discussed this with other people, I've found that the teachers who used humor well or the ones who created an enjoyable environment were remembered with the most detail. You may believe that you are only recollecting the stories or jokes or perhaps just the good times you had in those classes, but my own observations indicate otherwise. Beyond the good times the information gained when the mind is being stimulated in a non-threatening way is processed deeply. Even though recall of specific details may be less than perfect, the data are utilized by your brain and accessed quite readily in a wide range of associative capacities. Essentially, that means you've learned it, and you can use it.

For people with ADD the learning process *requires* a non-threatening environment. This is not the usual school setting.

What appears to be happening is a combination of positive experiences are working together to create an enhanced learning environment. Most obvious of these is the effective use of humor or pleasant experiences to resolve fears or concerns about the learning process. Intimidating material becomes anything from just less intimidating to outright pleasant. Fun. The happier you feel, the better you tend to put your into a reasonable perspective. Since fear itself is basically an irrational response (It's the exaggeration of caution.), then being relaxed and in a pleasant frame of mind automatically defeats some of the tendency toward irrationality.

Additionally, when learning is fun there are fewer inhibitions against it. And with ADD these inhibitions develop early. This is differentiated from fear in that the defensive response provoked by fear is global. If you are phobic about mathematics, then your preconceived notions make learning it painful if not impossible.

Inhibitions, however, are somewhat more specific. They can block the learning process without regard for subject matter. Or they can interfere with a certain teacher's ability to reach you. Or they can simply stop you from understanding a part of one area.

Inhibitions and fun are mutually exclusive experiences.

Think about the last time you were really enjoying yourself. Inherent in that experience is loosening up, that is, releasing inhibitions. An enjoyable learning environment releases fears and inhibitions and makes us *open to the experience of learning.*

We become receptive to the input of new knowledge.

Add to that the fact that the teacher is truly enjoying the experience and another inhibition disappears, the age old conflict between teacher and student. Instead of existing on either side of the learning fence, they coexist on the same side.

Once the entire process becomes pleasant and pleasing, enjoyable and fun, then can we get serious about learning.

To be sure initially it may mean many educators will need to learn how to use humor and how to be more relaxed. Techniques that encourage teachers and professors to relate more closely and more comfortably with their students will have to be developed. And nobody loses.

Certainly, ADD-affected students tend to improve their performance and productivity in environments in which they are having fun. An additional bonus is that other borderline students are likely to improve as well. Easily distracted students find themselves much less distracted and, therefore, more involved when they look forward to a positive and pleasant experience.

I often wonder how many hundreds of people are walking around with some of those astronomical facts ready to be accessed just because of Monty Python. Or, for that matter, what would my GPA have been like if History, Calculus, Anthropology and Zoology had been taught in something other than a monotone?

At teachers' conferences countless methods of capturing and keeping the students' attention are proposed. Rarely is the concept of fun, however, given credibility beyond the second grade.

I assume that's because those who are teaching teachers to teach presume it to be unnecessary.

Well, they're wrong.

CHAPTER FOURTEEN

Inside Getting Grades

Another book I'd like to write would be about the deleterious effect academic grades and the attitudes that surround them have had on both society and its citizens. For now, consider this chapter as a synopsis of the battle between grades and creativity with personal growth being sacrificed on the side.

"This is a test. Put your books on the floor and take out a piece of paper."

Those words chilled my bones for a quarter of a century. Read the following eight statements and decide how many are appropriate.

1. "Sure, I'm glad you got only one B, but why wasn't it an A?"

2. "I hate it when grades come out. My folks are never satisfied."

3. "I don't know why he hides his grades from us. We only want what's best for him."

4. "The reason I'm tough on him is so he'll achieve his potential. There's always room for improvement."

5. "Grades are the currency of your academic career."

6. "It's a tough world out there. She'll thank me later for having high expectations of her."

7. "I don't give out A's. An A means perfect knowledge of the subject and that's not very likely in this class."

8. "I guess I didn't pull my average up far enough so I lost my car privileges."

In 1996 President Clinton announced his decision to create a cash award merit scholarship program.

You get the grades, you get the money.

I wish life were that simple. So much for

helping the ADD population. A news commentator reminded us that disadvantaged kids have brains too. Did someone forget intelligent kids who have learning disorders? If you want to give cash awards, give them to the kids who are trying hardest.

Academic *performance, not the acquisition of knowledge nor the creative drive,* has become a national obsession. A radio ad proclaimed that when our national team competed in the international academic Olympics and came in fourteenth, there was no one there to cheer them. I directed my full attention to the radio. I listened intently to hear how by supporting these efforts regardless of where they come in we encourage our next generation to continue to strive regardless of whether they're first or fourteenth. Isn't continued effort without undue regard for specific results one of the qualities that made our nation great?

It never came.

The announcer went on to say, somewhat nonsequitorially, that we should (and I'm paraphrasing here) push these kids to become first because that's the only way we as a country are going to survive in the world economy. The implication being that less than first is a waste of effort. Completely missed was the most important point that we need to be supportive *regardless of outcome.*

If we take this radio announcement as well as the statements at the start of this chapter as truths, then you shouldn't go to a physician who didn't have the highest average in medical school.

You'd better check the college grades of your kids' teachers. Refuse to allow them to be taught by some second best teacher who didn't get A's.

If you're a successful business owner, but you didn't pull terrific grades, you have no business being successful.

Don't listen to beautiful music produced by non-valedictorians.

If that movie director didn't get an A in cinematography, boycott his movies.

If your investment counselor didn't get straight A's, you'll lose your shirt.

Sounds bizarre in this context, doesn't it? What's missing is that we have forgotten to reward the two elements of education that account for success in life. Creativity and drive. Both characteristics of many children and adults who have Attention Deficit Disorder.

I've worked with a lot of people who weren't A students and who've done damn well. Creativity can be defined as the ability to look at old things in new ways. Drive is simply the desire to create. Put those two together and stand back. It's not necessarily the A student who can do that either.

There's nothing wrong with getting A's. However, it only means that you can function within the structure of that one system, academics.

To function at life takes more. Creativity and drive. Unfortunately, there are precious few academic rewards for these life skills.

By the way, here's how to score the test at the beginning of this section: If you thought *any* of those statements were appropriate to getting a quality education, you've got some homework to do.

Because they're not.

CHAPTER FIFTEEN

Creating Balance Inside the ADD Mind

Deep inside all of us is the need for balance. We call it many things: harmony, inner peace, self-satisfaction. This particular inner conflict, trying to find balance, probably more than all the others, characterizes the ongoing existence of the ADD mind.

Consider this old riddle: "What is it that gets bigger the more you take away?" Aside from the obvious snide remarks about government, the answer is, of course, a hole. The theory being that a hole is nothing. It contains nothing, and the more you remove the more nothing you have. Or so the riddle goes.

Look at the converse. "What is it that gets smaller the more you add to it?" Being ADHD myself I've been pondering this in the spare time that I've created by avoiding sleep. Both riddles appear to be asking obviously impossible questions. You take away something, and something else is supposed to be diminished. You add to it, and it's augmented. Simple. The actual answer to the first riddle appears to be a trick of semantics. "A hole? Oh, I get it. Ha! Ha!"

Or so we imagine.

In the real universe there is a narrow margin wherein taking away actually diminishes and adding actually augments. When you step outside this margin of safety, the opposite becomes true, and the riddles become the rule rather than the exception.

Imagine the growth of a star. Under normal circumstances as a young potential star accretes (gathers) material, it gets increasingly denser until it ignites. It continues burning while balancing its

---

continued accretion with losses due to burning and other forces. At some point, though, excessive accretion will cause it to collapse, and theory has it that this becomes a black hole. Just like in the riddle. Except now the star is dead.

An earthly campfire is another good example. As you add fuel, the fire increases; take fuel away, and the fire goes out. However, if you've ever made a campfire, you know that adding too much wood all at once will also put the fire out. Similarly, removing wood can let more air in, and the fire can grow accordingly. Remove too much wood, and the fire's out again. Finding the balance between too little, enough and too much is what distinguishes experienced campers from neophytes. This also is an excellent metaphor for the universe, and on a more intimate scale, for Attention Deficit Disorder.

As I considered this new way to look at those riddles, I began to notice an increasing number of things to which this applied.

Food. We need it, but too much or too little will kill us.

Oxygen. Oxygen toxicity (too much) and anoxia (too little) are both real life-threatening problems.

It even holds true for more abstract concepts. Love. It's been said over and over again that there can never be enough love, yet I've worked with numerous relationships in which one party felt smothered while the other felt ignored. Perhaps love requires a balance too.

When we demand too much of a relationship, it can be smothered, extinguished. When we ignore it or take it for granted, we get the same result. In a love relationship there is a necessary balance that must be found between being together and giving someone their own space. Too much in either direction and you are either smothering or ignoring. In every love relationship I've seen, each partner either learns to understand their own needs as well as their partner's, or the relationship will not survive. Find out how much space your partner needs, then give it.

That's the taking away part. Find out how much attention is needed and what kind, then give that.

That's the adding part. Imagine both partners doing this, recognizing the balance between letting someone do what they need to do to stay sane and being there to contribute when that's appropriate.

And while we're considering how much attention is needed, look at the application to ADHD. Here's a situation wherein the person with the attention deficit requires so much in the way of, ironically, attention that little else matters to them. It's worth repeating that the individual with ADD or ADHD has a profoundly compromised self-identity. Their inability to function in the manner expected by their schools, by their families, by society as a whole places them on the outside.

And they feel it. They devote most of their emotional energy to creating something, positive or negative, that they can call their own. Something they can attach their persona to and feel secure.

At very young ages it is painfully obvious that other kids are figuring out how to get attention as well as affection and approval. Despite the efforts of well-meaning adults and parents, quite often ADD kids do not experience the subjective feelings of attention, affection or approval. The mistakes that all kids make have repercussions on the ADD mind that sets them so far apart from the rest of their peers that it can't even be communicated. When disciplined, they will not be able to process the correction. The poor focusing, the lack of attention as it were, allows only the punishment to be processed. Cause and effect do not come together.

So they are punished. Even if that was not the intent, the experience for them is punitive, and while they may *intellectually* be able to verbalize cause and effect for your benefit, they experience repeated and personal abuse for two reasons. One, because they cannot link *emotionally* what they did with the punishment. Two, because they cannot make the crossover that would stop them from taking advantage of an opportunity to act out, they continue to act out seeking a stronger identity.

As destructive as this cycle appears, it persists because this is the reality in which both the ADHD and the ADD minds live. If we were all this way, such punitive measures would be replaced by more immediate and relevant corrections simply because both parties would be following the same interpretations of reality.

The non-ADD mind, because it does link together events that are further apart, struggles with understanding this relationship and interprets *their* observations within the scope of their own reality. *Hence, punishment is meted out that cannot possibly produce beneficial or positive results.*

We're back to balance.

Finding the balance between praise and discipline is essential. Too much of one and the other is rendered useless. Before you decide that this is true of everyone, do not forget that ADD *is in* almost everyone. It's an exaggeration of characteristics normally held in check by internal systems of balance. In a non-ADD person the balance between praise and discipline is a reasonably broad expanse. Many errors in judgment can be tolerated. ADD does not permit such tolerances. The margin of safety is narrow.

The balance, therefore, while delicate is discoverable because the ADD individual will direct you there. The profound and impelling need for a unique identity can be balanced against the need for approval.

Recognize and appreciate their uniqueness, and you provide that which they need most.

The most important aspect of who they are, therefore, is, ironically again, found within their deficits. The Attention Deficit Disorder mind is marked by a distinct deficit in the amount of attention *they feel they need*. It may be an ironic play on words, but it makes a critical point.

To find the balance observe the attention they don't have as compared to the attention they need. Compare also the deficits in the learning process with the deficits in their self-perceptions. Notice how intelligent many of these people appear to be then look at their dismal grades.

Furthermore, how many are "really nice kids" who can't seem to stay out of trouble?

This describes me, and it must describe countless thousands of others. I try to be proud of my accomplishments, but deep inside there's a feeling that I'm doing it wrong. That someone will discover my errors, and I'll be found out. I still fight for balance precariously perched like Tevye's Fiddler on the Roof.

Trying to balance my own observations of what is real against what appears to be the consensus of the rest of the world.

The ADD individual works hard for what they manage to create, but they do it in their own way, a way that is not generally acknowledged. Inwardly, they must balance who they believe themselves to be with who they thought they were supposed to become. Still seeking approval. Balancing and trying not to fall for on either side of their narrow perch awaits failure.

And the need for attention walks behind dogging our steps. How young most ADD kids must be when they learn that rejection, intended or not, is the most probable response to their seemingly unquenchable need.

Eventually, rather than seeking or even requesting attention other, more personally reliable behaviors, take root.

These may not be the most socially effective behaviors, but they work. The more attention they get, negative or not, the more proof they have of their effectiveness.

Such a balance may seem perverse to the non-ADD mind, but to the person inside it provides the security and ego strength they need so much.

CHAPTER SIXTEEN

Reducing Stress Inside the ADD Family

The concepts of being positive and finding balance should be reasonably well defined now. The further we look into the mind of ADD the greater the subtleties we'll find.

Another important characteristic of the ADD mind, however, isn't found in the individual. It's found as part of the group consciousness of the family. This dynamic contributes numerous new elements to the ADD mind that must be considered for our efforts into developing understanding to be truly productive.

Stress is only subtle until something forces you to confront it. Pigeon-holing is subtle even after you know it's happening.

Inside the family unit dependability and stability are requirements. Should one family member start to change or develop in a new direction, pressure is applied, often quite directly, to bring that person's behavior back in line.

As an example, children can react so strongly to divorce that when they become adults, they often maintain the fantasy that their parents will get back together. Once a new lifestyle is established, remarriage becomes another difficulty. Having adapted to a family structure, there is a profound inertial resistance to change.

Many of these stresses are just the opposite of what you might expect. If a family member succeeds in losing weight, there may very well be outward congratulations, the appearance of support. But it's not uncommon to discover the rest of the family suddenly eating richer desserts or even saying, "C'mon. One piece isn't going to kill you."

When I was a teenager, my mother needed to go back to work after my father died. I remember how encouraging I was on the outside. I even offered to drive her to and from work. Inside I was a mess.

I resented her change in status from full-time mother to business woman despite the fact that I was hardly home myself. Once I managed to adapt to that, I was horrified to discover she was developing a social life . . . with a man. I think I managed to sound pleased, but I was scared. At the time I had no idea of what, but that's what I felt, fear. Something was being taken away. Beyond the understanding that someone would be replacing my father and getting my mother's affection, there was a deeper more painful feeling that took me over a decade and a half to figure out. I wanted my dependable, stable mother just the way she always was.

It works two ways. As children grow up, they become more independent (hopefully). They challenge their limits and start exploring life. As parents we are supposed to wave goodbye with a smile on our faces. Most of us manage, but the smile does not eliminate the separation anxiety underneath. It has to be done, yet we don't like it.

As clinicians work with Attention Deficit Disorder, we observe their behaviors starting to change subtly. They become a little more responsive, more mature, within their family. Since these first few steps are quite small, they are usually suppressed by the same family members who are trying to help them. There's nothing malicious going on here. *Each member of the family needs all other members to remain constant.* This permits *one* individual to grow and change against a reassuring and stable background. That's quite a paradox. In order to grow, the rest of the family is expected to stagnate yet each family member feels the need for their own growth.

Often pigeon-holing sounds like jokes, "You've gotten so skinny, you're going to need a beer to keep your pants up." Sometimes it's sarcasm, "Look at who's so smart all of a sudden!" It can even be direct, "I liked you better the way you used to be." This even applies to friends and peer groups.

There's an underlying message that must not be ignored, "I need you so much that I'm afraid you won't be there for me when you change."

The solution is surprisingly simple. Whether you are doing the pigeon-holing or being pigeon-holed, be reassuring. *Actively* reassure your family members, and, as a result, yourself, of their importance in your life.

Do this often. The payback is immediate and immense.

CHAPTER SEVENTEEN

Implementing a Positive Environment

Finding just the right method of showing appreciation can be a full time job. You have to consider who you're appreciating, what you're appreciating, why you're appreciating it and, most of all, who you are in the equation.

The notion of giving praise and recognition is something we as a society have never been able to resolve successfully. As individuals, however, it's possible to create eddies of strengthening behaviors that fortify relationships even if the societal trend doesn't agree.

Now we need to work on rewarding correct behavior.

"For getting that A in History, I'm going to buy you that new baseball glove." Not a good idea.

"I'm so proud of you for being good this last month that you can have your own telephone." Another bad idea. Confused?

"If you don't fight with your sister tonight, I'll buy you both ice cream." Sound familiar?

"If you graduate from high school with a B average, I'll buy you a car."

The common threads in these four examples are:

     1) They're all rewards.

     2) They're all well-intended.

     3) They're all probably well-received.
and

     4) They're all wrong.

The focus, believe it or not, is not really on the accomplishment but on the reward. Even at that, the focus should go beyond the accomplishment to the person whose efforts made it happen

Even if you feel as if you had to sweat it out of them, the credit is still their's.

In one instance a child's mother actually took her six-year-old's hand and walked him over to where he had thrown his plate. Still holding his hand, she put the plate in his grasp, held it there, walked him back to the table and used his hand to place it where it belonged

By itself that sounds punitive. However, once the plate was on the table, she praised him for being so helpful and for being so grown up. She had to repeat that process only once more. The *next* time they had dinner, when he made it through without throwing his plate, she was right there with praise and love.

If you don't give credit where it's due, and where it's *needed*, especially with ADD, you run the risk of one of three unpleasant outcomes:

1) They lose their own identity in the quest for material possessions.

2) They transfer the need for love, affection and approval to the expectation of physical possessions.

3) They stabilize the national economy by assuming the trade deficit on their Visa card (or worse on your's).

If we're raised receiving goods for love (Sounds terrible that way, doesn't it?), then we grow up unclear about how to give or receive affection. Being a baby boomer myself, I know our parents literally went through hell for us and wanted to give us the best. In so doing we've developed a material focus unlike any prior generation.

Sadly, even when the family income is not as large or the home environment is not as nurturing, giving physical rewards is so much easier and so heavily reinforced by society that the pattern transcends social and class boundaries. We even measure the love of parents by the size of the gifts they bestow on their kids or on each other. Phooey.

Due partly to the trouble focusing and partly to an inability to control impulsive acts, the ADD mind with its generally low self-esteem and often poor grades in school causes these kids to challenge their relative value daily. By the time I have gotten to work with them, physical rewards of all kinds have been offered, given and taken back several times. I've had kids who have walked into my office confronting six months of being grounded with no allowance. I worked with someone who showered his kids with birthday gifts only to take them back one by one as they misbehaved until all the gifts were eventually gone. And he never caught on. His only comment was, "That'll teach them."

It didn't.

In learning to create a nurturing environment for ADD kids, I quickly discovered that the same suggestions can work for anyone. Each time we reward an accomplishment with a physical gift, we undermine that person's self-esteem. Just like other animals, if we're essentially trained to perform for a gift, then we eventually reach the point of "No gift, no performance." You can see this in children, teens, adults, horses, dogs and baboons.

Kids with ADD respond so beautifully to non-physical rewards that I had to try it with other people. Oddly enough not only did it work, but it shifted their focus *from the gift to their accomplishment and eventually to themselves.*

The secret to removing physical rewards is so

simple it's scary. It's so obvious we must have been looking the other way all these years. It's so effective that it alters the very nature of our communications.

"Hey, you did great!"

"I'm really proud of you."

"I couldn't have done that any better myself."

"You must feel pretty good. Great job!"

One warning: If you can't mean it when you say it, find something positive to say, anything, that you can say honestly. However, avoid reverse compliments and brutal honesty:

"It's about time you got that A."

"So you finally decided to hand in your homework. Think how good it would have been if you'd done that months ago!"

"I know you're not brilliant, but at least you're passing."

Anything that sounds like a compliment but still stings *isn't one*. Never allow yourself to resort to comments such as:

"Hey, I'm just trying to be honest." or

"He knows I'm just kidding!"

These are nothing more than statements of profound insecurity on the speaker's part. They are designed to *suppress* the desired activity or response.

There is no rationalization for the use of these comments or comments like them with anyone. Using them in ADD situations is guaranteed to set back your efforts.

CHAPTER EIGHTEEN

Inside the Mind
of a Winner

After all this talk about appreciating effort instead of being completely focused on outcome, this next chapter on winning may appear at first somewhat anomalous. Just as with the ADD mind, further exploration into any concept is required.

How each of us interprets the concept of winning determines the strength of our self-image. Being a winner is not so farfetched once the concept is embraceable.

There is a new ethic emerging that is certainly different. At first I thought it might be just another impediment society was throwing in the way of ADD. After looking at it more closely, it seems to be just the opposite.

I was raised with the "It's not whether you win or lose" philosophy. And, although we never managed to get really good at it, we learned that there was indeed some merit to enjoying the *process* of the game.

Unfortunately, the rest of society wasn't reinforcing this admirable ideal.

The profusion of sports events and international Olympic competitions has emphasized the need to come in first with such passion and such single-mindedness that "how you play the game" seemed to get a bit dimmer.

Interestingly, the change may not be all bad. I've certainly talked a lot about "second place is the first place loser." And I'm not disagreeing with the extent to which being number one has occluded reality. Perhaps we need to recognize that what we really want after all is that special type of feeling that can be had by being first or best. With this recognition comes the relief that accompanies finally being true to ourselves.

The trick is to get the feeling without the heart attack.

I was shopping in a Western store for a new headstall for one of our horses when I noticed some shirts with rodeo images on them. Now I'm not in favor of hurting animals, but I am attracted to rodeo events where the risk and challenge is absorbed by the cowboy. And I'm also attracted to romantic images of cowboys doin' their thing. (Thang?)

As I went through these shirts, I discovered they were decidedly different from anything I had ever seen.

"If I don't win, I won't play," proclaimed one.

"Winning isn't everything, but to hell with everything else," was another.

Bold and aggressive statements like these filled the rack. "I'm tired of tryin'. From now on I'm winnin'!" I even found one I bought that held special appeal for the ADD side of me. What was this stuff anyway? What happened to our gentle hippie ideals?

Maybe we finally got realistic.

But how do we handle the times when we don't come in first? Is this new ideal just a setup for a long term depression punctuated by occasional wins? I don't think so.

Actually, I think it's refreshing. But it does involve some serious self-examination. What is winning? Is it coming in first or can it also include overcoming personal obstacles? Can it include self-improvement? Shouldn't it also expand to describe successfully working within a team? If so, then a movement to bring the ADD part of life into the fold is afoot.

The true competition isn't out there. That's too easy. Just beating an opponent is a cop out on the real test of success.

When we confront our fears, we're dealing with the only true monsters that block our paths. For every hero we pedestalize, inside there's a person who overcame some personal demon who threatened to smother their self-belief.

From those who fail this valorous self-examination we get the people with ego issues. Co-workers who would rather attack you personally than learn to work together. Or so-called friends who are intimidated by your successes. In close relationships those who have succumbed to the demon block intimacy or start arguments as a means of avoiding true feelings.

But from those who pass the test, from those who look the serpent in the eye and learn that it is merely a reflection of their own doubts, from these people comes the kind of success we associate only with winners.

Self-confidence.

Fearless communicating.

Honesty without brutality.

Compassion.

Those who ride their steeds away from this battlefield a winner are the ones who haven't destroyed or dismembered the beast. They've ridden into battle and tamed it. They've learned to harness and redirect the awesome energy we reserve for self-directed ruthlessness and apply it to growing and living and loving.

They've found that in order to come in first, we

must come in first in our own lives. We need to have the nerve to shape our reality as we need it, but also to temper our efforts with self-awareness and self-appreciation.

Not the false self-appreciation of the inflated ego. The true self-appreciation of the person who has looked inside and is no longer afraid.

The shirt I found for myself, the one that reflected my own ADD so well, I didn't wear for a while. One night as I was putting my horse away I got a little sloppy and ended up spooking the herd. As I dragged myself to my feet (something I find myself doing all too often), I thought it was time to wear the shirt. The next day I put it on.

"If I can't get killed, it ain't no sport."

Inside each of us are prairies and mountains waiting to be explored. It takes strength to lift that saddle and desire to stay mounted. But it's ours if we want to win it. ADD or not, those are the facts. The prize is within, and the sweet victory is the rest of our lives.

We ride tall.
We ride often.
We may ride into danger.
And we ride to win.
For ourselves.

SECTION FOUR

Inside
the Mind
and Biofeedback

CHAPTER NINETEEN

Inside the Mind
of the ADD Student
or
The Terror of Learning

With this section and, specifically, this chapter starts exploration deep into understanding how the ADD sufferer, for in this context they do suffer, fits into school settings. Writing this next chapter was very emotional for me. In some ways it was cathartic, but in others it just brought me face-to-face with the truth, a truth I had been denying for a long time.

I have a lot of difficulty watching television or movies that use angst as the primary vehicle to develop the characters. Although this is a popular emotional additive to entertainment nowadays, I've lived so much of it everyday in school that any exposure resonates inside me. Watching angst recreates my own school pains which include family reactions which I perceived as rejection.

Putting this book together has been very helpful to me in bringing these feelings into focus where they can be dealt with. Part of my intent has been to provide an experience that offers a similar opportunity to ADD's and their support system.

He sits in class.

"What's the teacher saying now? Boy, this chair is uncomfortable. How's the clock doing? What? Only five minutes into the class! Oh, man, I'm never gonna make it to the end... What's that she said? Ok, try to concentrate, this stuff's important. Look at Alice. She always knows what's going on. She always gets an A.

"I gotta focus. If I screw up another class, Dad says I lose weekend privileges. Focus on the teacher. Focus on the teacher."

"What, Mrs. Hardy? Uh, could you repeat the question? No, ma'am. I was listening. Yes, I'll try harder in the future."

"That was close. How come I never know the answer if everyone's telling me I'm so smart? If I'd only apply myself... I thought I was applying myself. Jeez, I don't know. I guess sitting at home staring out the window instead of doing homework isn't exactly what everyone else does. But I start out planning to do it.

"Oh, there I go again. What was she talking about this time? She's gonna ask me another

---

The A.D.D. Quest for Identity   **93**

question, and I'm gonna look like a dope. Not that that's anything new for me. How's the clock doing? Ten minutes?! This is endless! Oh. no! Here she comes again!"

"Yes, Mrs. Hardy. No, I don't know. Can I take a guess? No, I'm not trying to be a wiseguy, ma'am. No, I really have no idea. Yes, ma'am. I'll go to the Principal right now."

"Next time, I'm not even gonna bother going to class. I don't learn anything, and I just look like an idiot."

Looking inside the mind of Attention Deficit Disorder creates a new perspective for a lot of people. For a variety of reasons the ADD brain seeks continuous stimulation. It needs a steady stream of input and, if it's not forthcoming, the stimulation is created internally.

As a product of birth, children with ADD have brains that function generally at the higher end of the intelligence scale yet fall to the bottom end of the performance scale. There are two primary causes of ADD: genetic, the legacy of your parent's genes; and congenital, the product of unknown factors before birth.

Interestingly, it appears to be more common among adopted children. Genetics as an explanation for this is not going to work so that leaves congenital. Since exploring the lives of large numbers of women who are planning to give a baby up for adoption and then following the adopted child would be prohibitively complex, finding the connection between adoption and ADD will be virtually impossible in the near future.

Fetal Alcohol Syndrome (FAS) may play a role in this population. This does not mean that these women are alcoholics, merely that they may be misinformed about the effects of alcohol or drugs on fetal development. Babies born shortly after WWII may have been affected by FAS since it was apparently not uncommon for mothers to have alcohol and tobacco during pregnancy to help them relax. This was probably the cause of my own ADD.

This is where biofeedback fits in. Regardless of the cause, it is now possible to train the brains of many people affected by ADD to create a more normal focusing ability. This makes it an exciting addition to the arsenal of drugs and behavioral therapies.

Even as I write this, I've been diverted by a dozen things that could be better put off until tomorrow. Finally, I've dragged my brain back to the task at hand with the consummate rationalization that what I had actually done for the past two hours was take a break.

"Now, where was I?", my mind searches for a thread of continuity amongst the barrage of potentially diverting input. *"Oh, yes, Chapter 19!"*,

As I search through the files on my computer, I see we have defined both the syndrome and the problem fairly extensively.

Now we get to talk about solutions.

CHAPTER TWENTY

Defining the ADD Student
and
Defining a Solution

Many people report great relief at simply finding a name describing the conditions that affect them. Even better is learning there are others who share your problem thus validating this part of your reality. Perhaps best of all is discovering processes that can mitigate the condition and its impact.

Research is finally catching up with the issue of ADD.

This chapter describes the opening of a doorway on a solution to this frustrating and pervasive problem.

See if you can identify with any of these statements:

"Whenever I start a class, I feel like I'm a week behind. It's like everyone else knows what's going on except me."

Here's another one: "Everyone says I'm lazy so I guess I am. I don't *think* I'm lazy."

I'll give you one more: "I don't know why I've always gotta be different, I just do. I just like being a maverick."

It's obvious by now that these are ADD statements. People who can relate well with these statements probably have a history of struggling through school not to mention difficulty dealing with authority figures. Until the last ten years or so they might have been labelled as having one or more of a variety of dysfunctions.

Learning Disability is the least noxious of this group of dysfunctions. Antisocial, under-achiever, juvenile delinquent or, my personal favorite, minimal brain dysfunction were applied to these people as society itself struggled with a serious problem that came to light as Western Civilization emerged from World War Two.

Here's the ADD list of accomplishments from

the non-ADD perspective:

Some seemingly bright kids just go bad.
They don't work in school.
They resist authority.
They refuse to fit in.
They don't pay attention.
They've always got a dozen projects of
one kind or another started but
none get finished.
They're the "Jacks of all trades, Masters
of none".
They flunked out of school, but they can
rebuild an engine perfectly.
They can't pass Math, but they can run a
drug selling ring.
They can't sit still in class, but they can sit
for hours programming a computer.
Their attention span can be as brief as a
few seconds.
They cannot control impulsiveness.
Their self-identity is very poor.
And they're generally very bright.

But they can't fit into the academic world in which they traditionally do poorly. If somehow they make it through school into the adult world, they'll survive and may even do very well. But the structured scholastic environment for these people is more often than not anathema.

Remember, if you can identify with any of this, don't be surprised. These symptoms are shared by a considerable portion of the population because ADD shows up as exaggerations of existing characteristics.

Everyone has had problems controlling impulses at some time in their lives. People with

ADD experience this practically constantly common for our minds to wander in class to time or in a class that you don't particula you've got ADD you lose track even interested. Most people have felt like they I in at least a few times in their lives.

With ADD you're lucky if you find someplace to fit in at all.

Since discovering that I have ADD (Actually I think it's ADHD based on my need to always be doing something.), two very important changes have occurred in my life.

First, I finally discovered why I did so poorly in school. I had gotten tired of being told, "You could do so well if you'd just apply yourself."

I thought I had been.

If I could have done better, I would have. The fact is my motivation was strong. I wanted desperately to please my parents and all those teachers. I just couldn't. By the time I got to high school, I really believed I was lazy. My father had told me repeatedly that once I found myself I'd do fine. I had given up on that ever happening. But finding out that there was some explanation made a difference.

Second, I decided to study what little was known about this new disorder. As it turned out, research was just then involved in looking at the brain waves of people with ADD. Anomalies in certain electroencephalographic (EEG) patterns were showing up that seemed to be associated with the condition, and some researchers were even using biofeedback to work with it.

Now there was an explanation *and* a treatment.

Over the past decade other advances in behavioral management of ADD have been made. It's now possible to identify ADD and ADHD through the use of EEG technology.

It started as a nightmare.

Thousands, probably millions, of bright and creative people have been pushed aside. For the first time, it's changing. All we need now is time. Eventually, we'll reach the so-called lazy kids, the ones who never really fit in, and bring them back. More importantly, we'll be helping them find their identities.

And we'll all reap the rewards.

CHAPTER TWENTY-ONE

Developing a Solution

I was lucky enough to be in graduate school at the dawn of clinical biofeedback. I just happened to be studying the subjects that put me in repeated contact with people doing research in the area. At the time I had no idea if this was leading to something that would turn science around or if it was just a laboratory oddity. When the clinical applications started turning up, it was still labelled as a fad that would have no real clinical value.

That was in the mid-70's. A mere ten years later the biofeedback research on ADD began to develop serious momentum. The excitement over the diagnosis which explained so much kept interest alive in the research.

When I was a graduate student, there was a continuing argument between the physiology and psychology departments. The psych grads tended to view the body as "a complex life support system for the brain." Some of them even added "the brain is nothing more than housing for the mind." Well, these were fighting words for us physiologists, even a stress physiologist such as I was. Despite the fact that studies in stress had to involve psychology, we approached the brain, and indeed the mind, as an integral part of the body indistinguishable from the millions of biochemical reactions that sustain life . . . indistinguishable from life itself.

The brain, the mind, the body . . . all one.

In recent years those psychology and physiology grads have come together on this. One of the areas of research that catalyzed this joining of minds was the development of brainwave biofeedback.

This reborn field called EEG Biofeedback or Neurofeedback positively affects Attention Deficit Disorder and Hyperactivity. So I want to take the time to explain the basis for its effectiveness.

EEG Biofeedback goes all the way back to the beginnings of biofeedback. In the late '60s very simple amplifiers were measuring brainwaves and filtering out all but the alpha waves. If you made alpha waves when hooked up to one of these devices, you heard a sound, and *that* was your biofeedback.

Since alpha waves were associated with quiet states, it was assumed that by learning to do this at will you could create a better quiet state. To say this was a little naive would be an understatement, but we said it and did it just the same.

I found that I could make alpha waves by doing all sorts of things other than just sitting and thinking. Hence, I spent a good deal of my time at Colorado State attached to a massive device in a biofeedback laboratory. Today such a device would probably fit on a thumbtack. Anyway, I discovered that I could roll my eyes up as far as they could go and produce prodigious amounts of alpha all the while believing that I was getting in touch with myself.

The headaches alone should have told me something.

Anyway, it turned out to be more complex than we imagined. The strength of the waves had to be taken into account as well as the differences in the function of the waves depending on which of 23 combinations of placements you used for the electrodes. The early equipment wasn't able to process multiple waveforms, not to mention strengthening one specific wave by a certain amount while suppressing another and still monitoring the whole wave spectrum for signature patterns.

Come to think of it, I'm probably lucky I didn't get biofeedbacked from a lightning bolt considering some of the special protections added to modern equipment that weren't even thought of at that time.

The A.D.D. Quest for Identity　　　　　　　　**103**

Recent advances in technology permit this intricate and specialized biofeedback to be done with absolute safety. And sophisticated applications like ADD, panic disorders and head injury rehabilitation have become available.

In these applications parts of the brain have been identified that produce waves differing from individuals unaffected by those problems. For example, in panic disorders and head injury rehabilitation, a certain combination of alpha and theta waves in specific parts of the brain seems to enhance the anxiety state.

By training individuals to reduce the alpha waves while sustaining the thetas, reductions in anxiety reactions and return to normal waveforms are being reported.

The same thing is true of ADD. Enhancing beta wave production while inhibiting theta wave energy in the area around the Rolandic Fissure of the brain seems to be improving focusing while decreasing impulsiveness.

So today I can rationalize that those endless hours in graduate school with my eyes rolled up avoiding the real world were moments of brilliance justified in the name of science and not just another ADD ploy to avoid schoolwork.

Maybe.

CHAPTER TWENTY-TWO

THE USE OF
EEG BIOFEEDBACK
(NEUROFEEDBACK)
IN
ATTENTION
DEFICIT/HYPERACTIVITY
DISORDER

The following is a technical article that I wrote about the application of biofeedback technology to Attention Deficit Disorder. This article discusses the first effective direct methodology for both identification and treatment. At the end of this article are six technical references which will direct you to the seminal research from which these methods were developed.

1. Understanding the Disorder

Both Attention Deficit Disorder (ADD) and Attention Deficit Hyperactivity Disorder (ADHD) are characterized by the inability to focus as well as a variety of behavioral problems including excessive impulsiveness, defiance, inattentiveness and risk-taking behaviors. In the early twentieth century, this collection of symptoms has been treated as a grouping of behavioral issues called Minimal Brain Dysfunction which was assumed to be untreatable. Later it was referred to as Learning Disorder and was treated from a purely behavioral perspective. (Lubar, 1991). A large number of children with ADD or ADHD, *and subsequently adults,* mostly male, have fallen into the unfortunate category of "under-achievers" with the mistaken belief that they have been refusing to use their intellect to best advantage.

The strict behavioral model has never provided adequate answers for therapeutic interventions. Prior to 1970 both sedatives and stimulants were utilized with varying results. Eventually, the use of methylphenidate HCl (Ritalin) came to be recognized as the standard treatment for ADHD. The fact that such a stimulant was producing a calming effect as well as a stabilizing response in children gave weight to the theory that the children were suffering from something with more than a behavioral etiology. As the area of Learning Disorders was explored more fully, the diagnoses of ADD and ADHD were designated for this specific symptom group.

2. Theory Behind the Technique

Combining the facts that Ritalin had a stabilizing influence with the growing awareness of familial trends especially along the male lines caused researchers to speculate about possible organic causes. It was theorized that some region of the brain needed internal stimulation as in a feedback loop and was receiving this from the stimulant effect of the Ritalin. It was assumed that without this internal stimulation, the individual would seek stimulation elsewhere and consequently be unable to hold a focus on any single event. The stimulation of a constantly changing environment appeared to be required.

The creators of the television show, Sesame Street, discovered that rapidly changing informational systems resulted in greater retention and increased interest in the subject matter with concomitant decreases in distractibility. If the specific brain activity responsible for these problems and the improved responses could be identified, then it might be possible to more accurately diagnose and treat these children. Furthermore, it was theorized that it might be possible to train them to modify the functioning of those areas of the brain in which the problems showed up.

3. Scientific Evidence

Research has recently shown a strong biological basis for ADD and ADHD. Both PET Scan (Positron Emission Tomography) and SPECT (Single Photon Emission Computed Tomography) have already demonstrated both cortical as well as subcortical abnormalities in the brains of children and adults with ADD and ADHD.

In 1992, Mann *et al.* published findings showing excessive slow activity in the EEG of individuals with ADD. The presence of this slow activity follows the distribution reported by Zametkin *et al.*(1990) using PET Scan. In addition, children with ADD and ADHD show even more EEG slowing and lack of fast beta wave activation during various academic tasks such as reading, drawing, listening, mathematical computations, puzzle completion and others. One way of looking at the degree of slowing in the EEG is to examine the ratio of slow theta activity to beta activity over different cortical locations. The highest concentration of excessive theta activity relative to beta is usually found along the midline between the sensory motor cortices near the Rolandic Fissure.

Tansey (1990) showed that training individuals to normalize brainwave signatures in these regions showed improved WISC-R (intelligence) profiles as well as "significant remediation of the learning disorders."

4. How a Biofeedback Program Works and What To Expect

Following an extensive evaluation to identify both the behavioral and EEG pattern dysfunctions as well as the probability of effective response to the EEG biofeedback systems, the individual starts the first phase of the training program. This encompasses about 10 sessions of working with computer-driven biofeedback of their brainwaves. During the biofeedback sessions when a more normal brain wave response occurs, a recognition signal is produced thus teaching the individual when the stronger patterns are happening in their brain. During the first 10 sessions, appropriate training responses are identified which will indicate the probability of success in the long run.

The second phase is the bulk of the training period and can take an additional 30 to 45 sessions. As the training proceeds, behavioral changes generally start to be seen by both family and teachers. Appointments are commonly scheduled twice weekly during this period and support discussions with the family and patient are strongly advised.

The final phase sets the pattern as permanently as possible by gradually working with the individual less often. The tapering process covers about 15 to 20 appointments spread out decreasingly over several months.

Each session includes both EEG biofeedback

---

and behavioral suggestions designed to enhance the effect of the training. Family members of both children and adults receiving EEG biofeedback are strongly encouraged to be as involved in the process as possible since their interactions can provide a powerful reinforcement for the developing behaviors as they occur.

5. Explanations For Typical Behaviors

The two most obvious symptoms affecting people with ADD and ADHD are poor focusing and distractibility. With poor focusing the mind seems to wander aimlessly in a dreamy, nonspecific manner. On the other hand distractibility is characterized by several thoughts struggling for top priority simultaneously.

Clinically, there seem to be two general types of patterns in both ADD and ADHD. One pattern is manifested by increased theta wave production whenever a task requiring focusing is attempted. This produces an increase in the theta/beta ratio with a concomitant decrease in clear focusing capability. In one clinical case, a young man actually fell asleep in a wide range of circumstances which precluded simple boredom as an explanation. This was often misinterpreted as oppositional behavior and caused him to get in trouble on a regular basis. What was occurring was a dramatic increase in theta activity when he attempted to focus which subverted conscious activity driving him into a sleep pattern.

The other pattern typically displays reduced beta activity either at all times or specifically when challenged with a focusing task. In these situations the reduction of beta in the 16 - 20 Hz range also carries into the SMR (sensorimotor rhythm) range of 12 - 16 Hz. Reductions in SMR are generally accompanied by increased activity levels as the individual seeks stimulation. Under these circumstances a highly distractable state is produced and studying or learning is dramatically compromised.

In both types of patterns there is a reduction of self-esteem that creates numerous secondary and tertiary problems as the normal struggle for identity becomes greatly exaggerated with continuous evidence that failure is imminent. Frustration becomes a way of life with rage and temper outbursts occurring with surprising force.

6. Conclusions

EEG biofeedback has been scientifically and clinically proven to be an effective aid in the treatment of attention deficit disorder and attention deficit hyperactivity disorder when used to train reduced theta wave activity and enhanced beta wave activity in the regions over the Rolandic Fissure. A full evaluation is required as well as cooperation of family members to maximize the potential of a program. Additionally, EEG biofeedback can be an alternative when medication is contra-indicated or a conjunctive aid when medication is being used.

An important consideration when working with ADD and ADHD is the method by which the signals for focusing are processed in the brain. It appears that the early cortical messages indicating increased focusing on visual and/or auditory input are translated into poor focusing or distractibility based on whether theta is enhanced or beta suppressed. Neurofeedback (EEG Biofeedback) entails reversing these trends.

Reports from hundreds of clinics around the country indicate virtually uniformly positive successes. At The Biofeedback Center in Reno improvements in all age ranges have been seen from 8 to over 60 years.

7. References

Lubar, Joel F., M.O.Smartwood, J.N.Smartwood and P.H.O'Donnell (1995). Evaluation of the effectiveness of EEG neurofeedback training for ADHD in a clinical setting as measured by changes in T.O.V.A. scores, behavioral ratings, and WISC-R performance. *Biofeedback and Self-Regulation, 20:1*, 83-99.

Lubar, Joel F. (1991). Discourse on the development of EEG diagnostics and biofeedback for attention deficit/hyperactivity disorders. *Biofeedback and Self-Regulation, 16:3*, 201-225.

Lubar, Judith O. and Joel F. Lubar (1984). Electroencephalographic biofeedback of SMR and beta for treatment of attention deficit disorders in a clinical setting. *Biofeedback and Self-Regulation, 9:1*, 1-23.

Mann, Christopher A., Joel F. Lubar, Andrew W. Zimmerman, Christopher A. Miller and Robert A.Muenchen (1992). Quantitative analysis of EEG in boys with attention-deficit-hyperactivity disorder: Controlled study with clinical implications. *Pediatric Neurology, 8:1*, 30-36.

Tansey, Michael A. (1990). Righting the rhythms of reason: EEG biofeedback training as a therapeutic modality in a clinical office setting. *Medical Psychotherapy, 3*, 57-68.

Zametkin, Alan J., *et al.* (1990). Cerebral glucose metabolism in adults with hyperactivity of childhood onset. *New England Journal of Medicine, 323:20*, 1362-1365.

The A.D.D. Quest for Identity

SECTION FIVE

Inside the ADD Mind
When the Negatives
Win

CHAPTER TWENTY-THREE

Fear Inside the Mind

There's a secret to this letter. I found writing it personally beneficial because it's actually from me. I'm fortunate to have this forum for these feelings. I hope that by reading this you find something meaningful as well.

A footnote to this open letter and to this whole section could be that had fortune or Divine intervention or something not been with me, I would be in a much worse place right now.

Dear Mom and Dad

and, for that matter, Dear Teachers,

It's important to me that you understand how I feel. It'll be years before I can talk about the things I'm thinking today, and by then the damage may already be done.

You see, I know I've developed a reputation as either a screw up or a bad kid.

I'm not.

I know that some of my teachers really don't know how to handle me. I see it in their eyes. I know I frustrate everyone at one time or another. I can feel it. I know so many people think I'm lazy. And I especially know how upsetting I can be to all of you. They said I tested positive for Attention Deficit Disorder so now I've got a label.

The thing is, I'm not trying to hurt anyone. When I sit down to do my homework, I have every intention of doing it.

At least I used to.

Something has happened. Now I look out my window. I start thinking about all kinds of stuff, things that make me feel good. Like the few things I do at school that work out. Like those times when I get a really good grade or when some extracurricular activity really clicks for me.

The strange thing is when that

happens I don't know why. It just happens. Even if it appears that I've really applied myself (I don't know what that means, but my teachers say it all the time.), I haven't. I just did something that felt right, felt good. And I have no idea how I did it or how to do it again.

Even while I'm writing this letter, my thoughts are being dragged away by the voices I hear next door, by the radio, by the conversation at lunch today, by the thousands of other thoughts vying for my attention. I shut my window but not before looking outside for a while. Because this letter is so important, I kept coming back to it even though it took hours to write.

About my homework: I know I put it off. And when I finally do it, half the time I just don't bother to hand it in. I'm tired of feeling stupid.

I'm tired of feeling like everyone else knows what's going on except me. I'm tired of asking questions in class only to have my teacher get angry because she just talked about "that very subject". I'm tired of everyone, and I mean everyone, thinking that I screw up on purpose.

Don't you think I'd rather get good grades than be made to feel stupid all the time?

Do you think I actually enjoy being punished for acting out or not doing things?

Maybe I do. The pressure to

perform the way you want me to makes me feel crazy.

My most frustrating problem is having to look in your faces when you ask me why I did something bad or wrong or got bad grades.

If I knew, I'd tell you.

It seems that at least with punishment I get acknowledged. I know that sounds crazy, but I always feel like I'm on the outside anyway.

And please don't tell me how bright I am. I've heard that so much, I just want to run away when you say it. If I'm so bright, why are my grades so bad?

And why is everyone always angry at me? I feel like all everyone does anymore is punish me. Well, I

---

found something I'm good at.

I can get grounded, lose privileges and get detention better than anyone. Sometimes you look like you're either going to cry or strangle me. That used to scare me. That used to make me feel like I was the worst kid around. I don't feel anything anymore when you do that. It's just another event in my confusing life.

If you could look inside my mind, you'd see a jumble of thoughts all running around screaming, "Think about ME!" And I do. I think about all of them. All the time. Lots of those thoughts feel really good to me. I feel like I could make some of those work out real well. Some of my ideas are pretty exciting to me. But it feels like no one's paying attention to me anymore.

Except to be angry.

You don't have to be angry at me. I'm already angry at myself. You don't have to punish me either. I'm doing that too.

What I need is reassurance.

I need to know that you trust me. It'll take some time for that to sink in, and I may test it, but, hey, it's been a long time living the other way for both of us. I need to know that despite all my so-called mess-ups you still respect me. I need this because I'm not sure how to respect myself. Most of all I need to know that you won't give up because every day I think about that very thing.

I feel lonely in a crowd because I'm always different. Trouble is I'm not different physically so everyone just expects me to do what they do.

I'm trying to do all the things you want me to, but I have to do them my way. When I do it your way, it just doesn't work for me.

But I am trying.

Just acknowledge that and eventually I'll hear it. Maybe we can work together. Maybe there's some way, not necessarily your's and not necessarily mine, that'll let me be as smart as you say I am.

Just don't give up.

Please.

CHAPTER TWENTY-FOUR

How to Get to the Wrong Side of the Law

Anti-social behaviors include, in our society anyway, impinging on the rights of others and denying the presence of laws as well as ignoring a variety of ethical and moral values. Countless explanations for these behavioral problems have been proposed ever since humanity has had to deal with them.

Possibly for the first time we have both explanations and the potential for true rehabilitation.

Here is one view on how the ADD portion of our population may find their way over to the wrong side.

What we call "civilization" is the greatest single stressor in human existence. We have created an environment that is hostile to our own species' most basic needs.

I'm happy to acknowledge our impressive evolutionary accomplishments over our Paleolithic forebears. In addition to longer lifespans we boast more height, less hair and straighter spines.

Perhaps the strangest side effect of civilization is that we're forced to surrender talents that served us well when we ran wild. If you are still running wild, this may not be as great an issue. For the rest of us, it is.

We're still stuck with the physiology we had thousands of years ago.

The fight or flight instinct, for example. Instead of using it to avoid rampaging mammoths, catch wild boar or walk farther for water, we suppress it and produce high blood pressure, headaches, ulcers and insomnia.

Each of these meant something different to our precivilized predecessors. Elevated blood pressure improved the body's response to physical threat. Headaches probably forced slowing down to let the body heal. Insomnia actually maintained a state of alertness that enhanced chances for survival.

In my work with people who have ADD it's

essential not to lose sight of the primary symptoms including easy distractibility, acting without thinking, difficulty seeing one task through and following an organized sequence of tasks and poor self-esteem.

All but the last were probably desirable in the earlier Paleolithic age when it was essential to be able to shift attention among several stimuli, when acting impulsively was life-saving as opposed to anti-social, when difficulty following an organized sequence meant you could respond well to changing priorities.

The quality of poor self-esteem, however, is a by-product of not functioning within civilization's expectations.

Few cave dwellers had to sit through dozens of lectures in basic algebra or the history of civilization. ADD may only be dysfunctional within the context of a civilization structured so that processing rapidly changing stimuli, indeed *needing* changing stimuli, is a disadvantage.

The people I've worked with are very bright regardless of IQ scores.

They are pleasant and gracious despite labels of social difficulties.

As they learn to teach their minds to function within civilization's expectations, their ADD creates new perspectives from which society benefits. The Renaissance encouraged people to develop a wide range of skills and abilities. We seem to be on the threshold of a New Renaissance. Of learning to appreciate old Uncle Frank who never could get through school but could do everything else.

I was thinking about this very subject on the way to work when I was pulled rudely from my reverie by the honk of the car behind me.

Normally, I wouldn't be able to repeat the colorful invectives directed at me for such colossal atrocities as not departing a green light soon enough or only doing 70 in a 65 zone, but this time was very different.

I had been called a Renaissance Man.

I'd heard this phrase before. I've even seen the movie, but that didn't generate a working definition. It depends on whether you spell the first word with a capital letter. Since the movie used it in the title, I couldn't tell.

My handy dandy electronic dictionary stated succinctly, "rebirth or revival; a renewal of life or prominence." I was hoping for something more profound. While it's always nice to recognize one's personal rebirthing, the romantic in me was looking for a deeper association with an earlier historic period. Apparently, Hollywood wasn't interested in history because the qualities of a Renaissance Man (with a capital "R") have nothing to do with the movie.

A capital "R" Renaissance Man conjures up images of a multiplicity of skills: fencing and painting, foreign languages and poetry, hand-to-hand combat and philosophy, science and music. More than simply experiencing rebirth, a Renaissance Man, or Woman in today's society, is interdisciplinary in all aspects of their lives. Directed by an inner drive to experience life and to create their own unique identity they cannot simply experience something once or in just one way. They need to see it from all angles. Then they'll want to move on to something else . . .

much to the consternation of their more modern, non-Renaissance friends and relatives.

It's the moving on, however, that seems to impart the most problems.

We've been trained to believe that the more you do, the worse you are at all of them. Find a spouse, a career and a home then live the same life every day until you either retire or expire.

Despite the obvious appeal of this scenario many of us just can't do it.

All the other stuff on the plate is so damn intriguing that we have to taste it. We want to know not only what's around the next curve, but what's behind those trees and over those mountains. (And we mix metaphors with unusual grace and competence.)

So who's doing all this jumping around?

It's the Sesame Street Generation. The ones who can't sit still through a long boring lecture but can play six instruments. They're intelligent but they turned in book reports that never really reflected the plot of the book. The nice kids who got in trouble anyway.

The portion of the population I'm describing is, once again, people with Attention Deficit Disorder. By now the symptoms are reasonably well-known. What's not routinely discussed is the Renaissance quality itself. The need to carve out a piece of everyone else's niche just to create some kind of identity.

The Jack's of All Trades, this group also represents a large chunk of some of the most creative people in society.

Who else would end up studying such a wide variety of subjects? Without ADD distracting our minds, redirecting our attention and forcing us to jump from opportunity to opportunity there would be precious few Renaissance People. The drive to learn is less a consideration than *the need to find out who we are.*

It's pretty obvious when you think about it. The people with ADD compulsively explore seemingly unrelated topics. Combine this with the need to have a unique self-identity, and society has a wellspring source for new ideas. Unfortunately, new ideas challenge the status quo, and those challenges are perceived as threats. Sadly, it's easier to discard a threat than to deal with it.

Just why we still torture them in school has more to do with convenience and fear than education. We insist on conformity because it *seems* to simplify the process. However, the *non*-conformists, most are likely our ADD's, are the ones who shape society. They just have to survive academia first. This might explain why the original Renaissance Men studied fighting in addition to creative thinking.

Many of the people with ADD find themselves defending their hard found uniqueness. It's not unusual for school age kids to feel the need to defend themselves physically. It's not a big jump from there to other even less socially acceptable applications of force. If that identity is allowed to develop, the direction this person will take will also be socially unacceptable.

Where will instant gratification be found?

Where can force or the threat of force be applied successfully?

If these kids don't manage to get into the military, then the other side of the law holds their most promising options.

CHAPTER TWENTY-FIVE

There's No Such Thing as Lazy

Before continuing with why people with ADD run afoul of the law, I'd like to take a close look at laziness as one of the ADD faults since it's often associated with people who end up in trouble.

Inherent in understanding the mind of ADD is dealing with the feeling that these are lazy people. Of all the tags and labels placed indelibly the application of "lazy" is both the most dangerous and the most inaccurate. Dangerous because after a while we believe it and inaccurate because we make up the busiest fraction of the population in our never ending efforts to improve or even find our self-identities.

I love my office.

It's cozy and quiet with a simple feel that envelopes me whenever I enter. For many years it had been my *sanctum sanctorum*, a safe place where I could explore my innermost thoughts. Or play a computer game. With ADD there is a strong need for such places where you can find and define a piece of your identity.

The trouble began when I started dreading entering.

For one whole year I had been feeling annoyance, even irritation, when I came in. For a while I couldn't explain it. One day, on entering, that answer came to me. Another aspect of my ADD, difficulty prioritizing, had caught up with me.

Each time I walked in, I was being greeted by a pile of papers that I had started two years earlier. This was to have been my temporary heap. I then moved on to my daily pile (which, to be honest, was a composite of a whole bunch of daily piles) festooning the front of the counter that was supposedly reserved for setting up appointments. Behind these were a chain of piles, each with its own unique quality (at least, in my mind).

I swore I knew the contents of each of these piles right down to the scrap of torn stationery with an old address I might need someday. (Now whose address was that . . .).

There were piles in the copy room, and long metastatic growths of perilously perched papers could be found extending over any and all open spaces in the kitchen. My private office housed a morass of meticulously forgotten computer information laced with journal articles and mail I needed to answer. My desk had accreted aggregate stacks in places that made it impossible for me to consult there. In order to send a fax I had to bury the phone.

Somehow, my office had become a mess.

It had surrendered itself to the pervasive forces of entropy and embraced chaos. Just *when* this had happened and *how*, I assumed would remain in the annals of unsolved mysteries. To my chagrin, I found both the when and the how and managed to find the who while I was at it.

It should be no surprise that my Attention Deficit Disorder was playing a key role here. The intriguing aspect of ADD as it relates to my messy office is that it provides an explanation for something that has been relegated to the descriptor, "lazy", up to now.

When someone with ADD is confronted with a simple task such as putting something away, several issues surface at once:

"Do I know where this goes?

"Do I want to figure this out or do something else?

"Why am I still holding this?

"Now there's *something more interesting!"*

And the item gets placed anywhere handy. Case closed.

After a while, these singular incidents leave moraine heaps which if explored produce data of archaeological, if not geological, value. Once again, the ADD mind surveys the mounds and thinks, *"I would really like to clean this up. Where should I begin?"*

Now, here's the principle difference between ADD and non-ADD minds: the ADD mind perceives all this discreetly distracting debris as *equally and simultaneously* important, all screaming for attention with one cacophonous voice. Each one poses a new challenge, a new opportunity, a new demand, a new tormenting *pressure*. The resulting conglomerate exerts a unique force on the ADD mind, and in response to the question, "Where should I begin?" comes the subconscious, "Aaaaarrrrgh!!!" This is immediately followed by a tactical psychic retreat leaving the piles distressingly intact.

It just *seems* that we ignore them. Believe me when I tell you that we're very much aware of the presence of the pile monsters lurking on every flat surface.

Folks with ADD are filled with the good intentions needed to organize. Unfortunately, each effort is met with the same, "Aaaaarrrrgh!!!" and nothing gets accomplished.

We're not lazy. We're constantly overwhelmed by a society that expects organization.

We're not lazy, because once we get started you can't tear us away. Of course, if you succeed in tearing us away, some geologic time may pass before we manage to get back to it.

We're not lazy. The concept itself doesn't

make sense. If we're avoiding something, there must be a reason. With this logic I can almost make the case that maybe more non-ADD's should learn to look at it *our* way.

Almost. But I won't.

My solution to my own supposed laziness was to declare an office organizing day with full staff attendance. On that portentous day I relinquished control to my staff, and they told me where to put things . . . until we had to stop for the day.

The greatly diminished piles that were left became the seeds for larger and more abundant piles that act as dust shields for flat surfaces everywhere.

I have devoted much energy to the study of the Zen concept of self-acceptance. Unfortunately, this has initiated an inner conflict for me.

My inner voice (which speaks fluent ADD) tells me to accept the way I am and live with my piles.

My societal voice says that some day I'll drown in a sea of self-acceptance.

I guess I'll find out . . . some day.

CHAPTER TWENTY-SIX

Inside the ADD Criminal Mind

This is the final analysis.

When all else fails, when we as a society cannot care for our individuals, when large percentages are allowed to fall through the cracks that we have created, then we've lost sight of the purpose and benefit of a social structure.

Do not confuse this with a call for socialism. Politics is not at issue. Abhorrent is the military concept of acceptable losses. When human life is at stake, any loss diminishes us all as it denotes not the failure of the individual but the inability of the society that bore that person to care for its own spawn.

Here then is an explanation for why ADD's find their way into crime.

What's the difference between an excuse and an explanation?

Elemental to an excuse is the characteristic of forgiveness. The belief that responsibility can be set aside, and life can continue as it had.

An explanation provides new information for future use that does not remove or set aside responsibility but rather enhances it.

That's the nature of the information that follows. Explanation, no excuses.

As we've discussed, Attention Deficit Disorder can be readily identified by understanding the group of symptoms that includes (but is not limited to) extremes of impulsivity, the inability to prioritize, a lack of understanding of cause and effect, low self-esteem, the need for immediate gratification, social immaturity and the tendency to be a maverick.

As we indicated in Chapter Two, males seem to be affected by ADD two to three times more often than females. When considering *ADHD* that ratio jumps up to males being affected four to six times more than females. More research is needed to determine whether ADD or ADHD is the greater source of criminal behavior, but there is an informal consensus that both have a higher incidence of problems with the law than that found in the general public.

The problems are commonly amplified by a society that has as its most basic rule the punishment of negative behaviors and the reward of only the most exceptional successes. This leaves most of society, let alone the ADD's, unrecognized, unacknowledged and, basically, unappreciated.

Success is supposed to be its own reward, but

---

the need for outside approval can be profound. Oddly, for much of this same group, those punishments which we prodigiously provide produce the same negative behaviors we're trying to squelch. The kids getting detention at school include a large proportion of repeaters who are eventually getting suspended. Ostensibly, the combination of public shame and parental pressure would then reverse the anti-social behavior.

Unfortunately, and this is well worth repeating, *many of these kids with low self-esteem manage to develop a strong identity based on getting in trouble.*

They may even be the chronically late, the ones who always talk in class or the class clowns. Very often they are bitter about being punished since they are not connecting their actions with the punishment.

Several people who have come to me for stress management have been victims of criminal behavior. They have mentioned that they have feared recrimination at the hands of their perpetrators for helping to catch and convict them. This is why the Secret Witness and Witness Protection programs exist. The perpetrators do not see the cause and effect connection of robbing or hurting someone and getting locked up. They do, however, see the shreds of their identity torn away by a society that hates them.

No wonder they retaliate.

Remember, no excuses, just explanations.

Look closely at criminal behavior. Their objective is generally to get something as quickly as possible with as little effort as possible. In return for this they may get money, our most highly prized status symbol, or peer identity which amounts to status itself.

Consider the ADD symptoms. Given someone with those characteristics, which way do you think is most likely for them to go?

A) Spend four years in high school, suffer four more through college, maybe get to go for another two or three years, then there are still no promises and certainly no kudos unless you're at the top?

B) Start selling cocaine to your friends tomorrow and get a few hundred bucks every day?

Therefore, in addressing the apparent tendencies toward both anti-social and criminal behaviors in individuals with Attention Deficit Disorder (with or without Hyperactivity), the two most outstanding characteristics of the disorder must be considered: low self-esteem and impulsivity.

As I noted above, in the ADD personality low self-esteem creates an environment in which virtually any identity that can be adopted is embraced. These people do *not* respond effectively to punitive measures. The measures themselves are absorbed into the persona and actually become an important aspect of their identity. Such individuals, despite their cognitive belief to the contrary, value the attention provided, however negative, by the courts, police, the judicial system, counselors and even family members. They may react at the moment as if those measures had the appropriate effect, but at the next opportunity the memory of their strengthened identity (i.e. with the negative measures incorporated) generally proves more potent.

The punitive measures become attractive. *Their need for some reassurance of their own effectiveness is so strong that they become seduced by the same elements designed to discourage them.*

Impulsivity in ADD produces behavior patterns in which advance knowledge of consequence plays an *insignificant* role. Such people can have the negative consequences of their actions explained in detail and will still be unable to control their impulsive drive without effective therapeutic intervention. Their momentary needs far outweigh the intellectual inhibitions that should be controlling those needs, and their behaviors become anti-social.

When both of these characteristics are combined in ADD, a substance abuser, for example, may understand the punishment for a second DUI but will be essentially powerless to effect reasonable controls when the opportunity presents itself. Similarly, other criminal acts can be regarded in this light. Punishment of these individuals will cause them to suffer but is unlikely to correct, and may even provoke, the problematic and dangerous behaviors in the light of such a powerful synergy.

Now that we have a way to identify and treat ADD by looking for specific brainwave patterns and retraining them with biofeedback and positive reinforcement, we have our first real opportunity at criminal rehabilitation. I'm not sure that the punitive system has ever worked on any large scale since the number of crimes seems to be increasing at a disproportionately faster rate than population growth. But I can't help wondering who we might be able to help *before* they rob another house or sell drugs to school kids or worse.

If we can look for the individuals who may

respond to this kind of therapy, an alternative to the endless expense of prison is at hand.

It's a new way of thinking, but I don't see anything either historically or on the horizon with more positive potential.

SECTION SIX

Three
Clinical
Observations

CHAPTER TWENTY-SEVEN

ADD and Sleep

This section contains three observations relating to ADD characteristics I have made within the context of my private practice. They have not been confirmed by other clinicians or researchers other than through casual conversation. I do, however, stand behind these observations as I would not have included them in this book had they not shown up repeatedly. Also, the techniques I describe have been proven in my office and anecdotally by parents of ADD kids to be effective.

The first is about the incidence of sleep dysfunction and ADD. Sleep is a limiting factor of life and modification of sleep quality alters how we feel about everything.

My own clinical observations and subjective experience have demonstrated the importance of such potent elements as positive reinforcement, self-identity, self-image, intellect, and creativity as motive forces for those of us who have Attention Deficit Disorder, but I would like to devote some energy to describing some of my observations that perhaps may be somewhat more on the fringe. Actually, I prefer the term, cutting edge. Same thing, it just sounds better.

Being on the cutting edge, I would hope, would place these ideas in the category of things for which you can watch. I have observed these to be true in the context of my practice but have not as yet correlated them in the greater context of the general population.

I have observed that a disproportionately large group of people with ADD have a variety of sleep dysfunctions. As a group ADD seems to be a good correlate for insomnia. This does not seem to be discriminatory as to type such as delayed onset or interruptive, but there is the common thread of a generally lower desire to sleep.

It's as if with all the ideas and worries doing battle in the ADD mind sleeping would be a waste of precious time that could be better spent either developing ideas or fixing problems. That this could

---

develop, and probably has developed, into some forms of anxiety reaction and hence anxiety insomnia over time is undoubtedly true. But the etiology, the causative factor, would be the ADD.

The phenomenon of finding our minds spontaneously shifting into high gear as the mental relaxation that precedes deciding to go to bed comes over us is, as with so much of ADD, an exaggeration of a reasonably common problem.

In my practice I would estimate that these sleep problems occur about twice as frequently when associated with ADD.

Whether it's due to the over-activity of our minds or the continuing need to find expression for jumbled feelings is as yet uncertain. Whether the ADD mind truly perceives sleep as a threat of some sort that must be actively avoided is unclear.

But I have noted that there is a preference for wakefulness.

Problematically, this preference produces some serious side effects. Sleep is one of the four limiting factors of life. In Search & Rescue Academy we learned the Rule Of Three:

You can't live without air for more than three minutes.

You can't live without water for more than three days.

You can't live without food for more than three weeks.

Of course, these are guidelines, but you get the point. We need to add to this that you can't live without sleep for more than twelve days. (Maybe we can fit that into the Rule of Three by saying "three hundred hours.")

But the fact is that sleep deprivation produces some dramatic and serious symptoms: depression, delusions, dementia and death. The Four D's, as I learned in graduate school.

Compromised sleep *quality* can and does start you on this path, albeit more slowly. However, that slowness also makes it more insidious as reality shifts and the sleep compromised person does not realize that what is needed is better sleep.

Here, then, is another aspect of ADD. Already present is emotional lability due to the combination of ADD qualities that cause a negative reaction in society. Society's reaction provokes the self-belief that for the person with ADD they are less than or at least less effective than everyone else.

This emotional build-up is then exacerbated by poor sleep which introduces further tendencies toward depression and even delusory feelings that they are unliked, unloved and ineffective.

Getting the person with ADD to acknowledge this may be difficult. Indeed, getting the people within their support system to consider this could be just as hard.

With a child positive reinforcement becomes a reasonable technique once again.

"You look so much better after that full night's sleep."

Come to think of it, this is probably effective with an adult as well.

"I know you had a difficult night, but I think getting to bed a little earlier might have helped."

The A.D.D. Quest for Identity　　　　**147**

Be supportive, be understanding. If sleep avoidance has been a long standing habit, try to acknowledge how they feel and work *with* it. Starting arguments about when bedtime is *will* be counter-productive.

In any event simply understanding that sleep quality could be an important factor in ADD, and especially in ADHD, might give you an edge with which you can work. A possibility would be to discuss this with your family physician and consider medication *for a while*.

Then work on improving attitudes toward sleep with the objective in mind of decreasing and stopping the medication in a reasonable amount of time.

CHAPTER TWENTY-EIGHT

Motivational Problems

This next chapter addresses the question of what motivates someone with ADD and, conversely, what slows them down. The simple response that it is all due to the ADD perception of life is too pat and subject to the basic fallacy of assumption. I have noticed frequently the ADD phenomenon of someone with all F's suddenly and paradoxically getting A's in one subject. And then never have it show up again.

This chapter explores that phenomenon with what I believe is a valid and useful explanation.

Another unique characteristic of ADD that I have observed is sporadic motivation. No matter how hard you try to get someone with ADD to respond to urgency to get most things finished, they procrastinate.

And it's done with great finesse and expertise.

Unless it's something that stimulates them.

Usually, procrastination is a function of avoidance. Unpleasant tasks or events are seemingly pushed away by not thinking about them or at least by not acting on them.

If we're already not able to perform up to an expected standard, then it follows that we're not going to look forward to experiences that place us in a position to perform poorly.

Poor grades feel like ridicule and, in far too many instances, really are. Being called on in class can be humiliating if you're not prepared, and, if your past experience is painfully redolent of feeling foolish or stupid, the preparation itself becomes increasingly difficult.

A new pattern, one that has the *illusion* of protecting us, becomes stronger than the expected one of participating in classwork, homework, and tests. We actually become motivated *not* to attempt to perform in the belief that avoidance will somehow protect us from the unpleasant outcome.

Strangely most people with ADD have a remarkable peculiarity.

In truth, I suspect that what I am about to discuss is true of *all* ADD's.

There seems to be a pattern that, much to the intense frustration of family members and teachers, the ADD individual will suddenly and for no apparent reason perform outstandingly in one or two areas. In school the appearance of A's against a backdrop of D's and F's is disturbing to everyone, the student included.

Until recently it had been assumed that the catalyst was lots of stimulation and immediate gratification, as in a computer game. Yet not all people with ADD are hung up on computer games. And not all stimuli are as intense as a computer game.

What seems to be happening is that the ADD responds more to the *emotional* content of the event or subject than to what we interpret as stimulation. Once again, the need for identity creates the greater demand and literally anything could become the stimulus.

This circumstance covers the entire spectrum of potential experience. I discovered a predilection for music. For me getting an A in a music class was almost a given. I have no idea how or why I was able to do it, but I did. (Well, I have a theory which I'll get to in a moment.)

I would get an A in a music class and my teachers and parents would intone, "If you'd just do what you do in Music in History!"

And I would sit there and listen as if they were talking in some foreign language because I was completely clueless as to what I had done.

Perhaps we could call this *The ADD Stare*. That look that comes over kids when you're trying to motivate them and both of you know it's not working and it's most likely not going to work.

The repartee continues predictably, "Are you listening to me?" By this time you're probably trying to break out of this pattern but are powerless to stop following the script.

"Yeah, I'm listening."

"You are *not*. If you were listening, you'd start studying and pull those grades up!"

"I *do* study!!!"

"You call *that* studying?! You call sitting at your desk fiddling with your pencil studying?!"

"Look, I don't know what's bugging you, but get off my case! I'm doing the best I can!"

"Best? Best!?! Come on! I know you're not stupid, but you'd never be able to tell by your grades!"

"If everyone would just leave me alone, I'll do it my way."

"Your way? OK, how'd you get that A in music?"

"I don't know. I just did. I *like* music. It's easy . . . and it's fun."

"You know, everything in life isn't going to be fun. Most of the time you're just going to have to buckle down and *make* yourself do it. If you don't get the grades, you'll never amount to anything."

By this time our ADD student could transfer the negative feelings from his other classes to Music and even those grades could suffer.

The question I've asked myself is: Why some things are self-motivated and work out well, and other things that are externally motivated don't?

I have a good friend who is decidedly *not* ADD. She was describing how she went through Law School.

"Whenever I had a class I didn't like, I'd just make myself sit down and learn the material."

When she said that to me, it was as if I had heard it for the first time. For the first time I realized that I could never do that and I had assumed that this was true for everyone. It had not occurred to me that most people can just study something and learn it because they have to.

Just because a teacher said, "Learn this," they can go home and learn it.

That is definitely *not* an ADD characteristic.

If you don't like it, or at the very least, if you don't have some kind of appreciation for it, it's just not going to happen. You can hammer away at it for hours or days with good intentions and accomplish nothing.

I recall in graduate school loading my system with strong coffee to study advanced biochemistry. I liked the subject well enough but there was a rumor that the professor gave you a grade based on your major and not your performance. Biochemistry majors would be eligible for the A's; chemistry majors would get the B's; physics got the C's; and everyone else got D's.

I didn't want to believe this, but it worried me. I studied arduously for the first test. Since I still liked biochemistry, I managed to absorb most of the material.

I got a D on the test.

Disagreeing with the professor got me nowhere. A D in graduate school is very bad. I had studied in good faith and even after getting my test back I thought I had done well.

The next test was a little harder to study for. I did less advance preparation and more last minute cramming. The coffee seemed to be less potent.

I got another D.

I really thought I knew the subject. At least I knew it better than a D.

Studying for the next test was virtually impossible. Even with countless cups of coffee in my system, I kept falling asleep. I finally gave up at about 3 AM.

I got another D.

I didn't even bother studying for the last test which I failed. I was called before my committee who admonished me that I was not showing the proper commitment. After that studying for anything became next to impossible.

If I liked the subject or not, the strong negatives placed on me eroded my self-confidence and self-image. I cared about what my committee thought of me and apparently they thought very little.

Or so I interpreted it to mean.

We'll never know the truth. What is relevant is that my motivation for a subject I thought I was pretty good at shifted, and my grades dropped summarily.

Somehow I survived, but the path was torturous and circuitous with no indications of where it was headed. Another book, perhaps. I wish I could say that my survival was the product of never giving up, of good old American stick-to-it-iveness.

It wasn't.

I survived by a combination of serendipity and fear that I couldn't succeed at anything outside of school.

This attitude seems to be a very common occurrence with ADD. It often results in dropping out of school, but I'd guess that only occurs when dropping out is perceived as a viable option.

Since I have a background in physiology, I tend to approach problems such as this one physiologically.

It's possible that self-motivated issues being more emotionally guided are directed through deeper regions of the brain such as the limbic system which mediates many emotional responses. Externally motivated issues such as being told to do something you don't really want to are more intellectual and may be more cerebrocortical in nature. That is, they would be mediated by the cortex or exterior of the brain.

Deep brain responses may have a higher priority or simply more associative neurons firing in response to the stimulus. Therefore, the deeper, more emotional response will provide more sense of self and will result in stronger positive feelings such as survival, approval or identity.

It has already been shown that we tend to emphasize those things which improve our chances for survival or our capacity for approval or strengthen our self-identity.

If this is true, then anything to which we can

---

attach a strong positive emotion and reasonably current forms of positive reinforcement should produce improved studying in ADD.

In fact, this turns out to be the case.

Contrary to a popularly held belief that external stimulation needs to be diminished in order to get an ADD student to concentrate, the primary change needs to address the question of motivation and the emotional content of the motivating event.

As the student becomes aware that:

1) they can indeed do the work correctly,

2) they are not *regarded* as stupid,

3) there are no penalties for *doing* the work,

then internal motivation, the emotional kind, can begin to develop.

They can do the work correctly. This may involve considerable patience and probably much one-on-one tutoring. When tutoring, substitute exasperation and pleading or threatening with encouragement and gentle repetition. I'm well aware that you may be near the end of your rope, but giving in to easier and more pejorative behaviors *guarantees* you'll lose the student.

As they become aware that they can do it, the desire to continue will *slowly* surface. With the beginnings of self-motivation must come sincere and frequent positive reinforcement.

They are not regarded as stupid. The need for external validation, praise and approval is strong in all of us. In ADD it's essential. Once again, sincere approval is what's called for.

Help them recognize whatever degree of success they've made. Do not sully their pleasure by pointing out how much they have yet to do. *They* already know this. Let them learn to appreciate their accomplishments. by appreciating them together.

There are no penalties for *doing* the work. This may sound strange, but don't forget about compliments that sting. Avoid, "Now, you'd better keep that up!" or "It's about time!" or "Now that you can do it, I'm out of here. Finish it up before I get back!"

The best I've heard is the constant increases in the amount of work as the ADD student's performance improves. I understand the teachers' rationale for doing this, but imagine this from the ADD student's perspective: "My reward for finally doing all my work is to give me more than I can do. When I finally succeed, I'm punished with overwhelming expectations."

These statements may sound severe, but variations of these find their way into even the most normal house.

Motivation that's self-initiated develops at glacial speed. Whether with adults or children, ADD will tax your patience to the limit. Hopefully, the potential result will motivate you to persevere. Anyway, the other ways haven't worked so you know that going back to more punitive or restrictive measures will only make matters worse.

There's no direction left but forward, and *that's* an option I personally prefer.

CHAPTER TWENTY-NINE

Teaching and Tutoring the ADD Student and Some Input on Ritalin™

The temptation to write an entire book on this subject is so strong that this brief chapter may someday be the introduction to a book on teaching and tutoring people with ADD. It's a given that traditional teaching methodologies simply will not work with ADD. The label, "Special Ed," may or may not be all that much help based on who provides the special attention and how it is followed up.

With ADD tutoring is often a practical aid to schoolwork, but once again it depends on the tutor. Often, if there are no other support mechanisms in place such as those discussed in this book, even one-on-one tutoring will be met with profound frustration.

Here are some guidelines for education based on my observations of both children and adults as well as myself. Do not be misled by the simplicity of these approaches. I use them and have seen them work. They can make a substantial difference.

Once data are assimilated, the ability of most ADD students to process this information is anywhere from good to exceptional. It's easy to forget that their poor grades are decidedly *not* an indication of intelligence. For that matter it can practically be assumed that if both poor grades and ADD are present, the student's intelligence is substantially higher than performance would indicate.

Many methods for teaching and tutoring ADD students have been promoted with varying degrees of success and varying degrees of expense. I've found that there are a few basic techniques that, if used *consistently*, can greatly improve both the transfer of information to and the interest level of the student.

We'll start by eliminating some myths that can be obstructive:

Myth 1: ADD students require a room with little or no visual stimulation. The ADD mind is busy and if data are not available for it to work with from the environment, it will come up with new data all by itself. If the ADD mind is going to be busy, it's going to be busy regardless of the external environment.

Myth 2: Give ADD students lots of breaks while they're studying. I must admit that I fell for this one for a while too. On the surface it seems correct. Give the student time to refresh and start anew. Unfortunately, the refresh cycle seems to be more on the order of several times per minute as opposed to a couple of times an hour.

More important is to recall that when there is an emotional commitment, the ADD student will perform quite nicely in an almost compulsive manner for hours on end. It seems that the attentional portion of this dysfunction may be mitigated by internal emotional responses as discussed in some detail in Chapter 28.

Myth 3: Ritalin is the best tool for managing ADD. See Myth 4 before we discuss this one.

Myth 4: Ritalin should never be used.

Somewhere between these two extremes lies reality.

As with any drug, the least effective dose may be the most useful. If any of the side effects of reduced appetite, reduced sleep quality, increased nervousness or personality change occurs, the dose should be reduced or the use of the drug reconsidered.

A new approach to Ritalin (methylphenidate) has been to prescribe it three times a day, seven days a week for years on end. This is quite different from the more conservative approach of once or twice a day with a pause for weekends and summertime. I have been unsuccessful in getting a full explanation for the rationale behind the more aggressive dosing.

Considering the serious nature of the drug, I prefer to lean on the side of caution.

I brought Ritalin up here since it is at the heart

of many school controversies regarding ADD students. Many schools are advocating aggressive Ritalin use ostensibly to improve the ability of teachers to work with all their students and not be forced to focus on just one or two. Such decisions as these give me serious concern as a clinician, educator and parent that the cause of education is not being served.

Anyway, teaching and tutoring an ADD student involves getting to know the mind of ADD which you have already done if you've read this book sequentially. Once you have some comfort dealing with the thought process the methods described below will make much more sense.

Rule 1: Make sure the students know you are truly interested in helping them. They may act like they don't care, but they do. It may take repeated proofs, but it will pay off.

Rule 2: Make eye contact. This helps get the point across in Rule 1. It also draws their attention to you for a few moments during which time you can make a statement that will be heard. This would be a good time for some positive reinforcement.

Rule 3: Be animated about your subject. If you are clearly enjoying *both* your subject and the process of teaching your students, then the students will eventually pick up on this and become more interested.

Rule 4: Don't be afraid to digress. This is where ADD's shine. Allow some digression from time to time. Occasionally, try to link the digression to the subject you're teaching. Some of the time just let the digression hang out in space and come back to the subject after a while. The time spent on the digression will keep their interest and allow you to carry them back to the subject.

Straight didactic teaching not only doesn't work with ADD, my own informal conversations reveal that *most* people do not prefer the dry and boring approach to learning.

Rule 5: Repeat as often as necessary. This is perhaps more appropriate in a tutoring circumstance than a classroom, although I can still see applications. Repetition makes sure the spaces when you lost the ADD student get filled.

Rule 6: Each time you repeat yourself, act and speak as if you are saying it for the first time. Use no anger, no frustration and no negatives. Review being positive. Learn how to approach problems from many angles. Find new and different ways to present information.

Rule 7: Believe in yourself and believe in your student. There's a mind in there that, once reached, will respond to your attention by performing right before your eyes. Your students will never forget you because so few people take the time to reach them in this manner.

Since the ADD identity devotes so much energy to looking for something nurturing on which to latch, if you provide a solid and positive structure, both of you will be winners.

NOTE: Ritalin is the brand name for the drug, methylphenidate, and is a registered tradename of Ciba-Geigy Corporation.

SECTION SEVEN

Inside
Positive
Communication

CHAPTER THIRTY

The Impact of Time Pressure

Frequently overlooked as an important factor in understanding ADD is time, its perception and management.

Just why time is handled so poorly by people with ADD could be attributed to the fact that it is such a profoundly subjective experience. Each of us experiences the flow of time differently from other people and differently for each activity and mood.

Since ADD interferes with the cause-and-effect relationship by introducing impulsiveness, instant gratification and opportunism, concepts of time flow are necessarily altered dramatically to compensate.

Time was when most of my work was with simple cases of high blood pressure, chronic low back pain, insomnia or headaches. Time was when stress management was simply a matter of getting more time for yourself.

No more. Now the stresses in our lives have become so complex that any pressures affecting one part of your life affect all of it no matter what. And if you have ADD, this situation is compounded several times.

It gets even more complex.

If your work or school situation is less than satisfactory, your ability to deal with pain is less. If your home life is demanding more of your time and you don't have it to give, your ability to function effectively at work or school is less. Push on this side, and something pops out on the other. This has actually been true all along and for everybody, but with ADD there is very little margin for error. Even worse, that margin is shrinking rapidly as combinations of stressors ranging from the economy to health to the environment to family all vie for your full attention *simultaneously*.

A new kind of inflation is occurring, time inflation. A minute today just doesn't carry the weight it did when we were kids. "Gotta minute?' has been replaced by "Gotta rush!" We all feel it, and we're all responding. With ADD, time pressure is deadly because you're starting with a compromised time sense. Time exists only in the moment. Planning is extremely difficult. Not because you can't conceive of it. It just doesn't get beyond the conceptualization. As we have less and less time available, the pressure to accomplish more becomes overwhelming to the person with ADD. Loss of adequate time for someone who is trying to accomplish everything at once is a stressor of immense proportions.

The cause of this loss can be blamed on our ever-increasingly complex lives. The impact of this strange phenomenon is the reduced value of free time as all the other demands come crushing down on us expecting to receive full and undivided attention . . . RIGHT NOW.

If you're an adult, imagine you've got a school meeting about the new sex education program. Another meeting with the police about your neighborhood watch group is tonight. Medical appointments are scheduled in conflict with everything else. The car is recalled, again. The VCR needs to be fixed. The kids need to be picked up. Extra time is needed for tax preparation. Watch certain kinds of cholesterol in your diet. Exercise more to stay healthy. And when the dust finally starts to settle, it's time to take your car in for a smog inspection. Then you get to think about your next employee evaluation. For the most part these are all products of the last ten years.

If you're a teenager, imagine your homework assignments are building up. You may have done some, but those are still crumpled in the bottom of your back pack. You haven't prepared for the tests next week, and even though you probably won't study in advance, you feel the pressure of them coming up. Tomorrow at school you'll have to confront those jocks again. Then there's the matter of that girl you're dying to meet but can't get up the nerve which is just as well because you're afraid of what she'd say anyway. You have to deal with bumping into *her*. Just to round out the picture your parents are going to grill you about your grades and homework, and they're not buying the story about getting it all done at school anymore. Grades are coming up soon, and it's not going to be pretty.

Special time to be with your family, let alone to spend on yourself or to be with friends, shrinks seemingly before your eyes. Special time for yourself is a vague memory.

At least we're not bored.

In all my years of working with a wide range of stress disorders and Attention Deficit Disorder, the lack of nurturing and self-nurturing seems to be fundamental to practically all stress responses. Problems arise for which there are no solutions ready. And, as with the AIDS virus, we scramble desperately to find answers while looking over our shoulders for the next crisis to take a bite out of our respective rear ends.

I'm not that pessimistic, but it does paint a difficult picture.

Difficult, but *not* impossible.

There are numerous wonderful techniques for relaxing, but they won't help if you don't have the attitude, the nurturing, to back them up. I know you've heard a lot about maintaining a positive attitude, but take a moment to consider why there is so much being written about being positive. It's very likely that as a society we are suffering from the onslaught of dozens of unrelated stimuli such as those mentioned above, and we need reminders . . . often.

As if all this weren't enough to heap on your shoulders, other people whether friends or relations have there own problems, and the effect their problems have on them finds its way to you.

The personal ads in the classified section are filled with lonely people self-isolated by a combination of feeling that they don't fit in, fear of repeated rejection and just plain lack of time. Not only is there no time to meet people, but we're so injured by painful relationships we need a safer, easier way to do it. Teenagers who don't have access to such a venue as ads simply don't socialize.

In my work with kids and adults who have ADD, I find repeatedly that they are doing poorly in school or on the job despite being pretty intelligent. They can't stay focused on the material before them. Their minds keep wandering often to the pressures I've noted above no matter how hard they try to stay on task. I often wonder if this is a new problem simply because civilization has finally gotten too complex. Perhaps these "problems" weren't problems before but have become so due to our inherent difficulties adapting to the modern age.

We need a way to restore our lost self-images, the feeling that we know who we are despite the ridiculous events of current times. We need to feel secure in who we are.

Sometimes I think about the Marlboro man. I'm pretty sure he doesn't worry about whether his personal computer is going to be outdated or whether he's going to be late handing in his homework. Or Betty Crocker. . . it's inconceivable to think about her pondering the ramifications of sex education in the schools.

I know that's simplified, but try this for a solution. The negative stuff is out there. With no effort on your part, it's going to find you, and you're going to need to pay attention to it when it does. Start devoting effort to finding what's good in your life. Do it now. Check out the beautiful sky. (Yes, it's still out there.) Look at the scenery and smile. Think about your kids or your folks, then tell them how much they mean to you. Do something nice for yourself. (This does not require an expenditure of a lot of money.) Try taking a walk. Not for exercise. Just stroll along. Pet a puppy dog. Feed the ducks a bag of Fritos. Read a trashy novel. Encourage the ADD people you know to adopt this mode of living. Just as an experiment.

When you do these things, tell yourself how good they feel to you. Say it out loud. Share this information with a friend. For that matter, tell your friend how glad you are that you have them for a friend. We're all in this together, and if we stop noticing that the sun is shining because we're always watching the ground for potholes, the stressors will win.

Consider that even ADD may have a bright side. (It does.) Find in yourself the ability to consider a new point of view.

You know those irritating people who always seem to be happy? I think they might be our future teachers. Stop for a moment and listen to the music.

Smile, darn you, smile.

CHAPTER THIRTY-ONE

Miscommunications

Miscommunication is so routine that we hardly notice it.

Hardly.

So many errors in our lives that we attribute to hostility or hostile intent are nothing more than miscommunication. Imagine that happening several times an hour every day with virtually everyone you know.

Welcome to yet another side of the mind of ADD.

Part of the development of language is the use of colloquialisms. These are the sayings and expressions that give considerable character to our communications if for no other reason than they are often difficult to understand. They usually remain as part of the spoken language and encourage much of the confusion and misinterpretation that is so common between us humans.

One such verbal gem used not exclusively by the ADD portion of the population is the expression, "Yeah, but..." Not only is this unique to our spoken language, it is inserted into a conversation so rapidly that both parties probably cannot recall it having been said. Yet its effect is felt, and the conversation wheels around it as if a pin had been stuck right at the spot the "Yeah, but..." was placed.

Do not be fooled by the seeming innocuous quality of this little expression. Its impact is evidenced by its ubiquitous presence. In ADD it's a tool essential to the special requirements of communication. The ability to agree and disagree simultaneously and painlessly provides you with the illusion that you're following a conversation that you may have lost five minutes earlier. Often just a "Yeah, but . . ." with a long vocal trail off will convince the other person in your discussion that you're carefully considering their words.

Here's an example: Jane says to Jim, her husband, "I *know* you can tell me how you feel. You don't have to keep it bottled up all the time. Can't you just try?" Jim responds with, you guessed it, "Yeah, but . . ." And stops talking in favor of shuffling his feet or some other body language indicating, "Change the subject."

It's fairly obvious what Jim is trying to communicate. "I don't want to do this." But there's more to it than that, and both Jane and, I'll bet, you, got the message.

Here's another one: Sue is talking to her daughter, Sally, "You know you should be doing your homework before you go out, shouldn't you?" Sally dutifully responds with the time-honored formula, "Yeah, but . . ." and petulantly goes to her room to stare out the window in ADD dismay.

Sally's communication is slightly more complex, even on the surface. Not only is she communicating, "I don't want to do this," but there's rebellion and self-identity wrapped up here. A n d there's more. While we may not be able to verbalize it, it can be felt. "Yeah, but . . ." is such a critical part of communicating, that there'd be considerable silence without it. ADD kids and adults have some difficulty controlling impulsivity even in the face of knowledge that contradicts the impulse.

For example: Alex has just been reprimanded for acting out in class as well as being late. Mrs. Brown, his teacher, has finished her reprimand with, "If you act out again, Alex, I'll be forced to report you. Do you understand what this means?"

Alex dutifully nods his head in agreement and

goes to his desk. Less than five minutes later he makes a disruptive comment that sends the whole class into hysterics. Mrs. Brown in her frustration says, "I thought you understood what would happen if you acted out again?" To which he has nothing else to say except "Yeah, but . . ."

The beauty of this idiomatic jewel is its ability to agree and disagree at the same time. "Yeah" mollifies the other party while "But . . ." sends the message, "I'm not going to comply." We get to retain our self-identity while acknowledging the authority or accuracy of the person we see as our adversary. In fact that's the principle issue, it identifies the interaction as adversarial and creates a defensive posture. While this shouldn't be necessary, our individual fears and insecurities dictate otherwise.

In the first case, Jim is afraid to open up to Jane, but cannot tell her this outright. Sally is telling her Mom that there's something else bothering her, but she needs help getting it out in the open. Finally, Alex, in a typical ADD quandary, is stating that he really has no idea why he does what he does and he'd stop if he could but he can't.

For two little words, they certainly can complicate our lives by blocking the real messages. If you feel this little idiom slip out, back up and try to speak what's really on your mind. It'll make a big difference in your relationships. Specifically in dealing with ADD . . . even your own.

I was discussing with a friend the possibility of writing a paper on this very subject, and he replied, "Yeah, George, I'd like to, but . . ."

What do you suppose he was really saying?

CHAPTER THIRTY-TWO

A Journey Inside
With My Son

Now we're defining the problem in more specific terms of what can be done. The stress response is so common in life that it cannot be ignored. Especially when discussing something with such far-reaching impact as ADD. Certainly, all of us can use some improvements in our stress management, but in the case of ADD the stresses are a little different and require a little extra attention.

As you read the next two chapters, I'd like you to think about what I consider the lesson I learned when I wrote them. At least as important as my desire to be an effective parent is my ability to be an effective observer. It is with our powers of observation that we benefit most from our journey inside the mind of ADD.

It is through the use of effective observation that we create accurate understanding and appreciation of what is happening in their world and bring it into focus with our own.

And, as the cycle continues, my children became my teachers again.

You'd think that with my background in stress management and Attention Deficit Disorder putting these two elements together would be simply a matter of course. Also, as you read this, you'll see once again how my children become my teachers.

I recall helping my son with his second grade spelling homework. "OK, Lewis, spell 'chase' for me." He paused sagely, "C-H-A- ." "Wait a minute," I proffered a fatherly suggestion, "*Say* the word first, *then* spell it, *then* say it again."

"Dad. That's *not* the way my teacher wants it."

"Let's do it this way anyway. You'll learn it quicker." By now, of course, quicker was out of the question.

"Dad. No. I'm just gonna spell it. C-H-A- ." Now my calm but stern father-knows-best persona was taking over.

"C'mon. Just say it first then spell it then say it again. We'll be done before you know it."

"Dad. I'm not going to do it that way. You're messing me up."

Somehow in his mind the strength and future of his self-image had became at risk here. Despite our pretty good relationship we were in a battle of wills. On a scale of one to ten his will is a fifteen. Butting heads was not a viable option.

I   considered   the   "I'm-the-professional"

approach, "Look. If you want to do this right, you'll just have to do it my way. *You* decide if you want a good grade." That didn't feel productive.

The "Dad's-been-around-too" approach had a certain appeal, "You think you know how to learn spelling? How many years of education has Dad had?" Always refer to yourself in the third person for strong parental impact. It's in the manual. I nixed this one too.

My deeper brain was anxious to use "the-demonstration-of-irrelevant-power" ploy. "JUST SIT DOWN AND DO THE SPELLING! GOT IT? GOOD!" In the nick of time one of my higher brain functions woke up and stopped me.

The situation would be out of hand in a moment. We were in DefCon 2 with bombers in the air when something happened. It had to be angelic intervention because what I did was not one of my usual responses.

I relaxed.

I sat at the table and waited for him to calm down. I didn't threaten him with, "You'd better get back to work if you want a story tonight, Mister." I didn't do anything. Not even a grimace came over my visage. I just relaxed. And within a few minutes so did he.

He came back to the table, "I tell you what, Dad. I'll *write* the words. OK?"

My response meant everything. Should I give in and surrender to his demands? My ego was standing up in the back of my consciousness screaming invectives. But my angel remained firm. I surprised both of us, "Sounds good to me."

And we did his spelling.

His ego remained intact. He only missed one word on his test. And we had a positive experience together.

Here's where the ADD and relaxation fit together. I realized that the harder we try to focus or work at something, if there's any anxiety involved, we lose ground.

We get sidetracked by ego issues.

Especially in ADD where self-identity is so fragile already. The need for a strong self-identity appears to take precedence over everything else.

Once anxiety is introduced, clear, logical thinking is out. I had been telling this all along to the kids with whom I work who have ADD.

But it's the first time I heard it.

SECTION EIGHT

How to be Positive with ADD

CHAPTER THIRTY-THREE
Two Rules to Live By

For the final chapter I chose to provide this information about being positive both as a constructive and practical note on which to end as well as a sort of summary since in essence these suggestions are the most critical aspect of ADD management.

The following is the information (slightly modified for this book) that I use in my office to assist people in understanding and implementing the principles of positive reinforcement and of being positive in general. This is as close to a step-by-step plan as I've seen for applying this concept to ADD. As with all these chapters, I've tried to keep it short and to the point which should make it easier to introduce into family life.

Besides, it would just feel better if everyone would learn how to relate in this manner.

By now it should be apparent that one of the most vital roles you could assume to assist someone with ADD would be to observe and reinforce the subtle changes in their behavior as they respond to your efforts and those of their environment.

These changes may appear spontaneously. Or, if they are going through a program of EEG Biofeedback, they may appear as a result of that therapy. It is also likely that your own efforts could be part of the provocation for growth.

In any event it is important for you to note these changes, however small they may be, and reinforce them since they are the seeds of the more dramatic developments for which we are striving. In doing this it may be necessary to examine a couple of the old methods and philosophies of parenting.

This may actually be the most difficult part of their development . . . your part.

Since ADD usually causes the individual to feel uncomfortably different from their peer group, it is reasonable to assume both self-image and self-esteem are probably quite low. Remember that in order to strengthen their sense of self-worth they may embrace practically any behavior they feel gives them some unique quality or some feeling of control over their environment.

This generally occurs below the level of consciousness.

By way of review, typically, these behaviors can appear as *anything*. Being chronically late, speaking out, being the class clown or even acting mean can give children and adolescents the image of having created an identity since these behaviors draw considerable attention to them. In fact, an identity of sorts, albeit a self-abusive one, *is* derived from these behaviors. They feel that in the eyes of their peers or even adults they have strengthened their individuality and given themselves the right to be a part of the same peer group or family support system they feel has left them behind.

Once again, don't forget that many of the normal corrective parenting responses are not only ineffective when applied to ADD (and, of course, ADHD), but they often have the unpleasant impact of *enhancing and encouraging* the negative behaviors we're trying to correct.

Positive behavioral corrections when combined with EEG Biofeedback are a wonderful and potent tool *if used consistently.* Even the positive behavioral corrections by themselves are far more potent than most people realize.

Normally, a customary correction to an inappropriate behavior might entail the removal or the threat of removal of something desirable. It's important to note that whatever is removed is often unrelated to the problem. Furthermore, the punishment *itself* may be delayed several days.

Consider these examples:

"If you don't clean up your room, you can't go out this weekend."

"When I get back, that homework had better be done!"

"When you get A's, you can have the car

back."

"You have to stop being late to get more privileges."

"When you act like an adult, I'll start treating you like one."

This is commonly accompanied by additional evidence of understandable parental frustration such as raised voices, severe threats or more extreme and inappropriate measures.

Just because you may be acting this way does not automatically make you a bad parent. You're normal. However, the special needs of ADD render these responses ineffective. Or even inflammatory.

For punitive measures to have effectiveness with ADD the punishment must be *relevant and immediate.* This is more complex than you might imagine and usually falls far short of being rendered accurately. Being grounded on the weekend *will* be experienced as punishment, but the *reason* for the punishment will be lost. All that remains for the individual is the reiteration that they are not valuable or important.

Therefore, and especially as an EEG Biofeedback program progresses, the continued use of these basically punitive and non-corrective measures can cause the improvements developing due to the biofeedback and your own efforts to regress and even disappear.

It is strongly recommended that parents and other family members as well as teachers try to utilize the following two approaches that summarize the entire perspective on ADD.

1) Punitive corrections need to be replaced with *positive reinforcement.* Regardless of the problem try to find something positive in their behavior, *anything*, and focus on that first.

"Even though you're still late, you're not as late as you have been. That's great."

"OK, I see you've made a start at cleaning up your room. It looks good."

"Hey, these C's sure beat those F's, and I've noticed you've been working harder. I'm proud of you."

This approach happens to benefit anyone *with or without ADD*, but it's essential with ADD.

And *be sincere*.

2) Diminish the use of physical bribes as rewards. Getting a physical gift for good grades, being on time, cleaning their room or acting responsibly has considerably less impact than the *emotional sincerity of true appreciation*. Both children and adults accustomed to physical rewards may take some time adapting to this, but patience and persistence, and of course consistency, pay off.

The well-intentioned use of rewards on your part may very well be reinforcing the wrong behaviors on your child's part.

The best demonstration of love is love itself.

These suggestions are beneficial to anyone with or without ADD. They can strengthen self-image and self-esteem dramatically for all family members.

Discuss these and other positive strategies with your family and even with the person with ADD. As a method of living, there's little to lose and everything to gain.

You have explored and experienced both the richness and confusion found in the mind of Attention Deficit Disorder. My hope is that you either found a doorway to understanding or a place of solace. While it would have been wonderful to write the definitive and complete work on ADD, my objectives were to bring to the light of day what is perceived as a frightening and mysterious mindset, and to prove that it is neither.

It's just different.

As a direct result of going through the effort of putting my thoughts in order for this book I found a portion of my own identity had been right in front of me.

ADHD.

I went to the local T-shirt store and had a special shirt made for me. On the front it says, "I'm not lazy. I'm just thinking." The letters, "ADHD", appear in red with a lightning bolt going through them. On the back, I placed my greatest discovery in large letters,

"ADHD AND PROUD"

About the Author
George H. Green, PhD, FABMP.

Four elements merge in Dr. George H. Green to create the unique perspectives he brings to his observations of people and relationships:
- His longstanding clinical career at The Biofeedback Center in Reno (*since 1976*) working with a wide range of stress disorders and Attention Deficit Disorder;
- His classroom teaching (*"Life Without Stress", Truckee Meadows Community College, since 1981*) based on the principle that learning should be both stimulating and fun;
- His continuing commitment to scientific research (While in graduate school four of his articles were published in scientific journals—see page 187. Currently, he is involved with other researchers studying the clinical results of EEG Biofeedback);
- His diverse background and interests which extend from his days as a professional musician in New York City to his current involvement with the Washoe County Sheriff's Mounted Posse.

A psychophysiologist, he holds and maintains several national board certifications: Biofeedback, EEG Biofeedback, Neurofeedback, Medical Psychotherapy and Hypnotherapy.

He has made Nevada his home since 1972 and has "substituted subways, crowds, humidity, museums and long commutes for mountains, horses, the desert and a ten-minute drive to the office. Out here I feel embraced by the culture."

Eclectic and dynamic, it is surprising he waited so long to write his first book, **Stop Being Manipulated** (*Berkley Publishing, 1995, ISBN 0-425-14686-3*). He says that now that he has started down this path, he plans to continue. **Life Without Stress: A Survival Guide**, Second Edition (ISBN 1-890669-00-8) proved it once. **The A.D.D. Quest for Identity: Inside the Mind of Attention Deficit Disorder** proves it again.

Other Publications by Dr. Green

Print Media:

Stop Being Manipulated, ISBN 0-425-14686-3, With Carolyn Cotter, M.B.A., 181 pgs, Berkley Publishing, New York, 1995

Life Without Stress: A Survival Guide, Second Edition, ISBN 1-890669-00-8, 198 pgs, The Biofeedback Center Press, Reno, 1995 & 1997

Life Without Stress, *The Newspaper Column*, SierraLife Section of The Reno Gazette-Journal since 1992

Videotape:

EEG Electrode Site Preparation, ISBN 1-890669-02-4, 29 mins., The Biofeedback Center, Reno, Autogenics Systems(distr.), Wood Dale, IL, 1995

The 10-20 System of Electrode Placement for Neurofeedback, ISBN 1-890669-03-2, 23 mins., The Biofeedback Center, Reno, Autogenics Systems (distr.), Wood Dale, IL, 1996

EEG Biofeedback Training, Tape 1: Beta-Theta and SMR, ISBN 1-890669-04-0, 75 mins., The Biofeedback Center, Reno, Autogenics Systems (distr.), Wood Dale, IL, 1997

Audiotape:

The 15-Minute Personal Growth Series: Initializing and Developing the Deeply Relaxed State, Volume One: Tapes I-VI, ISBN 1-890669-05-9, The Biofeedback Center Press, Reno, 1987, 1996

Scientific Research:

The Tetric Spiral: A Mind-Body Handbook, doctoral dissertation, private, 1983

Responses of heifers ingesting boron in water, with H.J.Weeth, Journal of Animal Science 46:812, 1977

Boron contamination from borosilicate glass, with C.R.Blincoe & H.J.Weeth, Journal of Agriculture & Food Chemistry 24:1245, 1976

Excretion of urinary free cortisol, with D.E.Johnson & J.J.Combs, Research Highlights of Colorado State University Experiment Station 948:42, 1975

Effects of boron-water, with M.D.Lott & H.J.Weeth. Proceedings of the Western Section of the American Society of Animal Science 24:254-258, 1973

Life Without Stress

A Survival Guide
Second Edition.

"Dr. Green's common sense approach makes *Life Without Stress: A Survival Guide* the most painless and stressless way to have, well, a *Life Without Stress*. If you need laughter, he'll take you there. If you need to cry, he'll be there crying with you. Based on his experiences and observations at The Biofeedback Center in Reno, *LWS:ASG* is at once sensitive, witty, direct, and most importantly, real. included in this volume are his personal and clinical experiences with Attention Deficit Disorder which make him an expert with true insight into this sensitive problem."

Catalog Reference: **LWS-1**   **ISBN1-890669-00-8**

Price: $11.95 U.S. ($15.55 CAN)

Send check or money order in the amount of $11.95 US plus $3 shipping to:

THE BIOFEEDBACK CENTER PRESS
3310 Smith Drive, Reno, NV 89509
Visa or Mastercard orders call:
(800) 310-7584 or (702) 825-0334

Prices and costs are subject to change without notice.

The 15-Minute Personal Growth Series - Volume One: Initializing and Developing the Deeply Relaxed State

This six tape set is comprised of images from actual hypnosis sessions with Dr. Green. The series of six images is arranged in increasing order of subjective complexity. The first tape directs you in detail into the relaxed state while succeeding tapes provide progressively less direction while dealing with increasingly subtle emotional experiences. This series is appropriate for use as an aid in stimulating personal growth or as a valuable tool in developing deeply relaxed states.

Catalog Reference: **PGS-1**   **ISBN 1-890669-05-9**

Price: $49.95 U.S. ($63.25 CAN)

Send check or money order in the amount of $49.95 US plus $4 shipping to:

THE BIOFEEDBACK CENTER PRESS
3310 Smith Drive, Reno, NV 89509
Visa or Mastercard orders call:
(800) 310-7584 or (702) 825-0334

Prices and costs are subject to change without notice.

Stop Being Manipulated:
How to Neutralize the Bullies, Bosses, and Brutes in Your Life

George H. Green, Ph.D. and Carolyn Cotter, M.B.A.
Published by Berkley Books, New York.

"Written by experts in psychology and business, *Stop Being Manipulated* explains 'The ABC's of the Manipulator'—revealing subtle forms of aggressive, controlling behavior and offering strategies that help you neutralize the manipulators in your life. This book can help you *stop being manipulated*—and rediscover the power to make your own choices *today*."

Catalog Reference: **SBM**   **ISBN0-425-14686-3**

Price: $5.99 U.S. ($7.80 CAN)

Send check or money order in the amount of $5.99 US plus $1 shipping to:

THE BiOFEEDBACK CENTER PRESS
3310 Smith Drive, Reno, NV 89509
Visa or Mastercard orders call:
(800) 310-7584 or (702) 825-0334

Prices and costs are subject to change without notice.

DATE DUE			
JY 24 '99			
JAN 2 3 2000			
MY 07 '00			
5·19·00			
ILL			
9732089			
6/29/00			
NO 27 '01			
OC 23 '02			
JY 06 '04			
OCT 13 2000			

GAYLORD   PRINTED IN U.S.A